THE
ALMANAC

FEBRUARY

M	T	W	T	F	S	S
					1	2
3	4	5	6	7	8	9
10	11	12	13	14	15	16
17	18	19	20	21	22	23
24	25	26	27	28	29	

APRIL

M	T	W	T	F	S	S
		1	2	3	4	5
6	7	8	9	10	11	12
13	14	15	16	17	18	19
20	21	22	23	24	25	26
27	28	29	30			

JUNE

M	T	W	T	F	S	S
1	2	3	4	5	6	7
8	9	10	11	12	13	14
15	16	17	18	19	20	21
22	23	24	25	26	27	28
29	30					

THE
ALMANAC

A SEASONAL GUIDE TO
2020

LIA LEENDERTZ

With illustrations by Julia McKenzie

MITCHELL BEAZLEY

An Hachette UK Company
www.hachette.co.uk

First published in Great Britain in 2019 by Mitchell Beazley,
an imprint of Octopus Publishing Group Ltd
Carmelite House
50 Victoria Embankment
London EC4Y 0DZ
www.octopusbooks.co.uk

ISBN 978-1-78472-521-1

A CIP catalogue record for this book is available from the British Library.

Printed and bound in the United Kingdom
10 9 8 7 6 5 4 3

Publishing Director: Stephanie Jackson
Creative Director: Jonathan Christie
Designer: Matt Cox at Newman+Eastwood
Editor: Ella Parsons
Copy Editor: Alison Wormleighton
Senior Production Manager: Peter Hunt

Ovens should be preheated to the specific temperature – if using a fan-assisted
oven, follow your oven manufacturer's instructions for adjusting the time
and the temperature. Pepper should be freshly ground black pepper unless
otherwise stated.

CONTENTS

INTRODUCTION

Welcome to *The Almanac: A Seasonal Guide to 2020*. This edition contains some old favourites – the tide, moon and sun tables, important dates, and happenings in the sky at night – plus some brand new features. This year, I have taken a close look at what goes on in and around our beautiful hedgerows every month. What flowers can we expect to see? What are the dormice and the linnets up to? What can we forage and when? I have added a new monthly sowing and planting table for the kitchen garden, and garden posy-picking prompts so that you always have a jam jar of something pretty and seasonal on your kitchen table. There are recipes to mark celebrations and seasonal food, from the first stems of forced rhubarb in January to a traditional carol singers' cake in December, and a new feature for this year is sauce of the month, to help you perfect your spicy barbecue sauce in June and your gravy at Christmas.

This edition also has a bit of a theme. The moon – with its monthly waxing and waning and its nightly passage through our skies – is a constant, magical reminder that we are a part of something larger. It has inspired poetry and folk song, and has great religious and spiritual significance. Both the words moon and month derive from the same Latin root, *mensis*, as it was once depended upon for keeping track of passing time and seasons, so a closer look at it fits neatly within the scope of this almanac. Look out for lunar references throughout, and use the moon timetables to track it across your own piece of sky.

The intention behind this almanac has always been to provide a set of keys to unlock various aspects of the seasons and help us all appreciate the moment we are in, rather than stumbling, blinkered, through the year. I hope that you will use these foragings, planet-spottings, songs, traditions, gardening tips and recipes to craft your own ways of celebrating, marking or just appreciating the year ahead as it unfolds.

Have a wonderful 2020.

Lia Leendertz

NOTES ON USING *THE ALMANAC*

Scope
The geographical scope of this almanac is the archipelagos of the British Isles and the Channel Islands or, to put it another way around, Great Britain and Northern Ireland, plus the Isle of Man, the Channel Islands and the Republic of Ireland. 'The British Isles' is used as shorthand, with apologies to the Channel Islands. The cultural scope of this almanac is the stories, songs, food and festivities of all the people who live in the British Isles.

The sky at night
The events within the sky at night sections generally fall into three categories: eclipses, meteor showers, and close approaches of the moon to a naked-eye planet, or of two naked-eye planets to each other. While the first two categories are self-explanatory, the third will benefit from a little clarification. The naked-eye planets are those planets that can be easily seen with the naked eye. They are generally very bright, as bright as the brightest stars, and this makes them relatively easy to spot, even in cities where sky-spotting conditions are not ideal. From brightest to dimmest they are Venus, Jupiter, Mars and Saturn. Those not included in this almanac are Mercury, Neptune and Uranus. Mercury is very hard to spot because it is close to the sun and therefore is usually lost in its glare. Neptune and Uranus can only be spotted with strong telescopes.

A 'close approach' means that two of them, or one of them plus the moon, are in the same part of the sky. They are, of course, nowhere near each other in reality, but to us, looking up, they appear as if they are. This can make them easier to spot than they would be when they are lone-ranging across the sky. To identify the part of the sky where they will most easily be seen, I have given the best time to spot them, plus a compass point and the altitude. The time is important, because the sky wheels around us as the night wears on. The altitude is given in degrees: the horizon is 0 degrees and straight up is 90 degrees, so find your point somewhere in between.

Tides

A full tide timetable is given each month for Dover. The table below gives examples of how you can make it work for you. Add or subtract these amounts of time from the tide you are interested in on the monthly table, and you will have the tide time for your particular location. For instance, if it is high tide at Dover at midday, it will be high tide at Bristol (−4h 10m) at 07.50 and at London Bridge (+2h 52m) at 14.52.

If your local port or beach is not featured here, just search online for 'tide difference on Dover', plus the name of your chosen spot, and then make a note of the difference on the tide pages for each month in this almanac. Note that these approximations provide a fairly rough idea of tide times, though they will be correct within ten minutes or so.

Aberdeen:	+2h 31m	Cork:	−5h 23m
Firth of Forth:	+3h 50m	Swansea:	−4h 50m
Port Glasgow:	+1h 32m	Bristol:	−4h 10m
Newcastle-upon-Tyne:	+4h 33m	London Bridge:	+2h 52m
Belfast Lough:	+0h 7m	Lyme Regis:	−4h 55m
Hull:	−4h 52m	Newquay:	−6h 4m
Liverpool:	+0h 14m	St Helier, Jersey:	−4h 55m

Do not use these where accuracy is critical: instead, you will need to buy a local tide timetable or subscribe to Easy Tide, www.ukho.gov.uk/easytide. Also note that no timetable will take into account the effects of wind and barometric pressure.

Spring and neap tide dates are also included. Spring tides are the most extreme of the month – the highest and lowest – and neap tides are the least extreme. Spring tides happen as a result of the pull that occurs when the sun, moon and earth are aligned. Alignment occurs at new moon and full moon, but the surge – the spring tide – is delayed because of the mass of water to be moved. It usually follows one to three days after. Knowledge of spring tides is particularly useful if you are a keen mudlark or beachcomber. You want a low spring tide for best revelations.

Gardening and fishing by the moon

Just as the moon moves the earth's water to create the tides, some believe that it has other effects on the natural world. If it can move oceans, perhaps it can move ground water, too, and even the water trapped in each plant. Planting by the moon is a method of gardening that taps into the the moon's phases. A new moon is considered a good time to sow root crops and those that are slow to germinate, because soil moisture is steadily increasing. Faster-germinating plants that crop above ground should be sown in the run-up to full moon, when the pull is strongest and so ground water is at its highest. The full moon is also the best time to harvest crops for immediate use, as they are at their juiciest. After that, the moon's pull starts to wane and ground water drops – these are good times for pruning (to minimise sap loss) and harvesting for storage (skins are drier and tougher). This year I have also included the best fishing dates, according to those who believe the moon has an effect on how likely fish are to bite. This almanac makes no claims on the efficacy of planting or fishing by the moon, but if you would like to give it a try, the relevant dates and jobs are included in each month.

Moon dates

The moon's phases have long been of great importance to many religions and beliefs, and astrologers believe that the new moon is the time for dreaming and making plans. So, throughout the book, you will find the dates that relate to each month's moon phases. Both the Hebrew (Jewish) and Islamic (Muslim) months begin at the sighting of each new crescent moon. However, the Hebrew calendar includes complex calculations and leap days to keep the months roughly at the same time each year, whereas the Islamic calendar is strictly lunar; therefore the Islamic month dates in this almanac are only predictions.

Note on the moon timetables: for ease of use, I have included just two columns – rise and set – for each day. On some days, moon set will occur before moonrise, so the times will not be in order. A dash denotes where the moonrise or moonset fall over midnight.

January

1 New Year's Day – bank holiday, England, Scotland, Wales, Northern Ireland, Republic of Ireland

2 Bank holiday, Scotland

5 Twelfth Night (Christian)

6 Epiphany/Three Kings' Day/Little Christmas (Christian)

6 Nollaig na mBan or Women's Christmas (Christian/Irish tradition)

6 Orthodox Christmas Eve (Orthodox)

7 Orthodox Christmas Day (Orthodox)

7 Lidat (Rastafarian)

13 Plough Monday (English tradition)

13 Lohri (Punjabi winter festival)

25 Chinese New Year – Year of the Rat begins

25 Burns Night (Scottish tradition)

29 Saraswati Puja/Vasant Panchami (Hindu spring festival)

THE MOON

Names for January's full moon – Wolf Moon, Stay Home Moon, Moon after Yule

The full moon on the 10th January will rise bright and clear over a bare, cold countryside, but just an hour later it will dim and may take on shades of pink. This is a penumbral eclipse (see page 15). You may hear it called a 'blood moon' – which sounds both dramatic and ancient, although it is, in fact, fairly recent eclipse nomenclature – but there are far older Celtic and medieval names attached to each month's full moon.

January's moon has several old names: Wolf Moon, from the time wolves howled particularly loudly to their packs through January nights; Stay Home Moon, a sensible idea in the cold and the frost and with all those wolves about; and Moon after Yule, which was given to the first full moon after the winter solstice.

When the full moon does climb out of the remnants of our shadow after 21.00 it will be bright and bluish, but it will illuminate very few nocturnal creatures. Almost all stay home this month, tucking themselves away to survive the cold.

The wolf's close relative the fox is one of the few that do not hibernate. It picks its way on moonlit January nights through stubbly fields and down chilly streets to find a meal, or calls in unearthly cries for its mate, just as the wolves would have done hundreds of years ago.

Moon phases

1st quarter – *3rd January, 04.45*

Full moon – *10th January, 19.21*

3rd quarter – *17th January, 12.58*

New moon – *24th January, 21.42*

Moonrise and set

	Lowestoft		*Dunquin*		
	Rise	Set	Rise	Set	
1st	11.30	22.36	12.19	23.27	
2nd	11.46	23.43	12.36	–	
3rd	12.02	–	12.51	00.34	1st quarter
4th	12.18	00.50	13.08	01.41	
5th	12.36	01.58	13.26	02.49	
6th	12.56	03.09	13.47	03.59	
7th	13.22	04.21	14.13	05.11	
8th	13.56	05.34	14.48	06.24	
9th	14.40	06.44	15.33	07.34	
10th	15.38	07.48	16.31	08.35	full moon
11th	16.49	08.40	17.42	09.29	
12th	18.08	09.22	19.01	10.11	
13th	19.32	09.54	20.25	10.43	
14th	20.57	10.20	21.49	11.09	
15th	22.20	10.42	23.12	11.31	
16th	23.42	11.02	–	11.52	
17th	–	11.22	00.34	12.11	3rd quarter
18th	01.03	11.42	01.54	12.32	
19th	02.23	12.06	03.14	12.56	
20th	03.42	12.34	04.31	13.25	
21st	05.56	13.09	05.46	14.00	
22nd	06.04	13.52	06.53	14.45	
23rd	07.02	14.46	07.51	15.39	
24th	07.49	15.48	08.37	16.41	new moon
25th	08.25	16.55	09.14	17.48	
26th	08.54	18.04	09.42	18.57	
27th	09.16	19.13	10.05	20.05	
28th	09.35	20.21	10.24	21.13	
29th	09.52	21.28	10.41	22.20	
30th	10.07	22.35	10.57	23.26	
31st	10.23	23.42	11.13	–	

Where moonset times are before moonrise times, this is the setting of the previous night's moon.

Gardening by the moon

New moon to 1st quarter: 1st–3rd and 24th–31st. Sow crops that develop below ground. Dig the soil.

1st quarter to full moon: 3rd–10th. Sow crops that develop above ground. Plant seedlings and young plants.

Full moon to 3rd quarter: 10th–17th. Harvest crops for immediate eating. Harvest fruit.

3rd quarter to new moon: 17th–24th. Prune. Harvest for storage. Fertilise and mulch the soil.

January moon dates

10th and 24th – new moon and full moon: best fishing days. Some fishermen believe that fish bite best in the 45 minutes either side of moonrise and set on the new and full moons. So that would be 90 minutes from 07.03 and 14.53 on the 10th, and from 07.04 and 15.03 on the 24th (Lowestoft times). **24th/25th – new moon: Chinese New Year.** The new moon that falls between 21st January and 20th February brings Chinese New Year, this year the Year of the Rat. Because of time differences, the new moon is on the 24th in the UK and the 25th in China this year, but will be celebrated on the 25th. **24th – new moon in Aquarius.** This month's new moon is in Aquarius, which astrologers believe is an unconventional and trailblazing sign that is helpful in bringing about change. You will see the fruits of this at the next full moon in Aquarius, on 3rd August. **26th (predicted) – day after the sighting of the new crescent moon: the start of Jumada al-Thani.** The sighting of the new crescent moon brings the start of the Islamic month Jumada al-Thani, also known as Jumaada al-Akhir. **27th – day after the calculated first sighting of the new crescent moon: the start of Shevat.** The crescent moon also marks the start of the Jewish month of Shevat. The name is thought to originate in a word meaning 'strike' and relates to the heavy rains the month can bring.

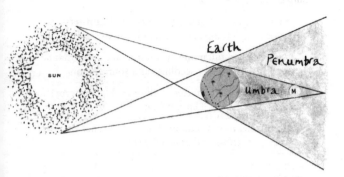

Penumbral eclipse

There will be a penumbral eclipse of the full moon on the 10th.
This means that the moon passes not through the full shadow
of the earth, but through the outer, shady bits (the penumbra)
just beyond it. The view from the moon would show the sun
partially sinking behind the earth, but never quite vanishing
completely. This eclipse should turn the moon dimmer and
with luck give it some shades of pink and red between 17.00
and 21.00, though there will be nothing as dramatic as we
would see with a full lunar eclipse, and it may just be an
anticlimactic dimming. A penumbral eclipse can only happen
during a full moon and when the earth, moon and sun are
almost but not quite aligned. Full alignment creates a much
more impressive, full eclipse.

THE SKY

At night

3rd and 4th: Quadrantids meteor shower. The sky will be dark from the half moon setting not long after midnight until 07.00. Best time for viewing will be around 04.00, when the radiant (the point from which the meteor shower appears to emanate) will be at an altitude of 50 degrees in the northeast.

10th: Penumbral eclipse of the moon. Rising in the northeast, a gradual darkening across the full moon begins at 17.00, reaches a maximum at 19.00 and ends at 21.00.

28th: Close approach of the moon and Venus, visible in the dusk from about 16.30 in the southwest at an altitude of 28 degrees, until setting at 20.00 in the west.

By day

Perihelion is the moment in the year at which the earth is closest to the sun. This falls on 5th January at 07.47, when the sun will be 147,091,144km away (compare with aphelion on 4th July, see page 148).

The sun reaches an altitude of 18 degrees in the London sky and 14 degrees in the Glasgow sky at midday on 21st January.

Day length increases by 1h 14m in Lowestoft, Suffolk, and by 1h 12m in Dunquin, Republic of Ireland.

Earliest sunrise: 31st January, Lowestoft 07.37, Dunquin 08.24.

Latest sunset: 31st January, Lowestoft 16.36, Dunquin 17.26.

Sunrise and set

	Lowestoft		*Dunquin*	
	Rise	Set	Rise	Set
1st	08.03	15.49	08.50	16.39
2nd	08.03	15.50	08.50	16.40
3rd	08.03	15.51	08.50	16.42
4th	08.03	15.52	08.50	16.43
5th	08.02	15.53	08.49	16.44
6th	08.02	15.55	08.49	16.45
7th	08.01	15.56	08.49	16.46
8th	08.01	15.57	08.48	16.48
9th	08.01	15.59	08.48	16.49
10th	08.00	16.00	08.47	16.51
11th	07.59	16.01	08.46	16.52
12th	07.59	16.03	08.46	16.53
13th	07.58	16.04	08.45	16.55
14th	07.57	16.06	08.44	16.57
15th	07.56	16.08	08.43	16.58
16th	07.55	16.09	08.43	17.00
17th	07.54	16.11	08.42	17.01
18th	07.53	16.13	08.41	17.03
19th	07.52	16.14	08.40	17.05
20th	07.51	16.16	08.39	17.06
21st	07.50	16.18	08.37	17.08
22nd	07.49	16.19	08.36	17.10
23rd	07.48	16.21	08.35	17.11
24th	07.46	16.23	08.34	17.13
25th	07.45	16.25	08.33	17.15
26th	07.44	16.27	08.31	17.17
27th	07.42	16.28	08.30	17.19
28th	07.41	16.30	08.29	17.20
29th	07.40	16.32	08.27	17.22
30th	07.38	16.34	08.26	17.24
31st	07.37	16.36	08.24	17.26

THE SEA

Average sea temperature

Ayr:	8.4°C
Sunderland:	7.4°C
Dingle:	10.3°C
Dublin:	9.6°C
Aberystwyth:	8.8°C
Lowestoft:	7.2°C
Poole:	9.7°C
Newquay:	10.4°C

Spring and neap tides

The spring tides are the most extreme tides of the month, with the highest rises and falls, and the neap tides are the least extreme, with the smallest. Exact timings vary around the coast, but expect them around the following dates:

Spring tides: 11th–12th and 26th–27th

Neap tides: 4th–5th and 19th–20th

In the tide timetable opposite, spring tides are shown with an asterisk.

January tide timetable for Dover

For guidance on how to convert this for your local area, see page 8.

	High water		*Low water*	
	Morning	Afternoon	Morning	Afternoon
1st	02.37	15.03	09.41	21.49
2nd	03.19	15.52	10.20	22.31
3rd	04.07	16.50	11.08	23.24
4th	05.06	17.56	–	12.11
5th	06.12	18.58	00.35	13.22
6th	07.14	19.53	01.52	14.27
7th	08.07	20.41	02.56	15.26
8th	08.54	21.25	03.53	16.19
9th	09.39	22.07	04.44	17.09
10th	10.23	22.49	05.32	17.57
11th*	11.06	23.32	06.18	18.43
12th*	11.50	–	07.05	19.28
13th	00.15	12.35	07.51	20.12
14th	01.00	13.21	08.37	20.55
15th	01.47	14.10	09.22	21.38
16th	02.38	15.04	10.08	22.24
17th	03.32	16.04	10.58	23.16
18th	04.33	17.14	11.54	–
19th	05.41	18.32	00.17	12.57
20th	06.59	19.45	01.25	14.04
21st	08.12	20.49	02.36	15.15
22nd	09.16	21.45	03.50	16.30
23rd	10.10	22.31	04.58	18.17
24th	10.55	23.11	05.52	17.30
25th	11.33	23.49	06.37	18.57
26th*	–	12.09	07.17	19.31
27th*	00.25	12.45	07.51	20.00
28th	01.01	13.18	08.20	20.25
29th	01.34	13.49	08.47	20.51
30th	02.02	14.17	09.14	21.21
31st	02.28	14.46	09.46	21.56

NATURE

The hedgerow in January

The hedgerow is asleep and so are its residents. There is some colour, from bramble leaves that still cling on in shades of yellow and purple, the trails of cold-dulled ivy and the battered leaves of evergreen hart's-tongue fern, but mostly all is bare, brown and twiggy. Hedgehogs are rolled up at its base, spines out, under piles of leaves and damp earth; hoverflies are secreted into hollow stems; seven-spotted ladybirds pile together for warmth in sheltered nooks and rolled-up leaves. The hazel dormouse snoozes in deep hibernation in its nest at the base of the hedgerow, safe from the ravaging winds and snow above. Badgers in setts dug below the hedgerow aren't actually hibernating, but they sleep more during the winter, and change is happening while they sleep. Badgers mate all year round, but because they have 'delayed implantation' it is only during this winter lull that the fertilised eggs are implanted into the womb and the snoozing female becomes pregnant.

Ivy berries start to turn black and ripen this month and are pounced upon by hungry starlings, thrushes and wood pigeons, who also take the last few holly berries. Bluetits will find galls and break them open to get at the larvae inside. These are lean times. But there are signs of life even now. The hazel catkins are elongating, kicking the year off. Lesser celandine and snowdrops start to appear along the hedgerow bottom.

THE FLOWER GARDEN

January's flower garden picking prompts

A few hellebore flowers floated on the surface of a small bowl of water (with a floating candle if you're feeling fancy); a fluff of old man's beard from the hedgerow with a sprig of witch hazel; a small twig of hazel catkins in a narrow vase.

Jobs in the flower garden

- Inside, sow sweet peas into long, thin pots or into toilet-roll inners stacked together and filled with compost – sweet peas like a lengthy and uninterrupted root run. Once they have germinated, transfer them outside and protect them from marauding mice by covering with wire mesh. Choose 'Matucana' for the best scent, or the Spencer series for big flowers and good fragrance this summer.

- Scented sprigs are one of the treats of the winter garden. Sarcococca is a brilliant little plant with shiny evergreen leaves that produces its sprays of citrus-scented blooms this month. Buy one and plant it and you will be filling the house with winter scent now and in many future Januaries.

- If you don't own any hellebores for floating, this is the time to rectify the situation, as you want to choose them when you can see the flowers. As long as the ground isn't frozen, you can plant them immediately, into soil you have enriched with compost, in a semi-shady spot. If you're not sure where to start, those known as Ashwood Garden Hybrids are particularly good, with clear colours and beautiful markings.

THE KITCHEN GARDEN

Cover clumps of rhubarb this month to force them and produce early tender pink stems about six weeks later. Buy and chit potatoes (leave them on a cool indoor windowsill to sprout) for planting out in spring. Chillies need to be sown in a heated propagator this month, but everything else can be sown in a greenhouse or on a windowsill without heat. This is a good time for planting fruit trees and bushes, if the ground isn't frozen.

Sowing and planting crops

Fruit/veg	Sow under cover	Sow direct	Plant
Chillies	✓*		
Swiss chard	✓		
Leeks	✓		
Onions	✓		
Broad beans	✓		
Hardy peas	✓		
Spinach	✓		
Radishes	✓		
Chervil	✓		
Parsley	✓		
Coriander	✓		
Apples			✓
Pears			✓
Currants			✓
Berries			✓

*In heated propagator

THE KITCHEN

Sauce of the month – brown butter

This is a comforting and very simple, nutty, buttery sauce.
Though it has a hundred uses, sweet and savoury (cook
scrambled eggs in it, finish steamed white fish with it, use it in
baking, pour it over popcorn, and so on), it is particularly good
at making something special of winter vegetables you may be
getting a little tired of. Try mixing it through steamed winter
greens just before serving, roasting carrots in it, or pouring a
pool of it over creamy mashed potatoes. Put 80g butter into a
small pan and heat over low heat until melted. The solids in the
butter will sink to the bottom of the pan. Heat without stirring
until these solids turn a nutty brown, then remove from the heat
and squeeze in the juice of one lemon. You can stop there and
use it just like that, or add a tablespoon of capers or a couple
of anchovy fillets. Use immediately or store in the refrigerator
(it will keep for a few days) and reheat before using.

In season

Vegetables: Brussels sprouts, kale, winter cabbages, Jerusalem
artichokes, celeriac, parsnips, salsify, swede, leeks, celery, chard,
perpetual spinach, winter lettuces, early purple sprouting
broccoli, and well-stored beetroot, carrots, garlic, onions,
winter squash and parsnips
Herbs: winter savory, parsley, chervil, coriander, rosemary,
bay, sage
Fruit: imported bergamot oranges, blood oranges, Seville
oranges, well-stored apples and pears, the very first forced
rhubarb
Meat: duck, pheasant, goose, woodcock, venison and hare
Fish: cod, whiting, Dover sole, haddock, pollock, bass, scallops,
mussels and oysters

RECIPES

Braised lentils with clementine roast carrots and mozzarella

Braised lentils are eaten for good luck in Italy on New Year's Day, the round shape of the lentils representing coins and wealth for the year ahead. Strictly speaking, the dish should be *cotechino con lenticchie*, lentils with *cotechino*, a big, fat, slow-cooked sausage served in slices atop the lentils, and you make a wish as you dig into a slice. But if you can't track this down, then serve it with whatever good sausages you can find, or make this vegetarian version.

Serves 4
Ingredients
For the lentils
1 onion, finely diced
1 large carrot, finely diced
6 tablespoons extra virgin olive oil
5 cloves garlic, crushed or finely chopped
250g Puy lentils, washed
1 small glass (125ml) red wine
About 750ml stock or water
1 bay leaf
½ tablespoon red wine vinegar, plus more to taste (optional)
Juice of 1 lemon
Large handful of chopped parsley leaves
Salt and pepper
For the carrots
2 clementines, unpeeled
4 large carrots (or equivalent smaller ones), topped and tailed and quartered or halved into long batons

3 tablespoons extra virgin olive oil

1 tablespoon fennel seeds

Salt and pepper

For the topping

2 balls mozzarella, torn into pieces

2 tablespoons extra virgin olive oil

Method

To cook the lentils, gently cook the diced onion and carrot in the olive oil until they are soft and translucent. Give this stage plenty of time as it informs the flavour of the whole dish. Add the garlic and cook for a few minutes more. Tip in the lentils, mixing them into the oil, then add the wine. Turn up the heat, stirring the bubbling mixture until the wine has mostly been absorbed by the lentils. Add the stock or water and the bay leaf, bring to the boil, and then reduce to a simmer. Simmer for around an hour, adding more water if necessary. The lentils are cooked when they are soft but still hold their shape. Season with plenty of salt and pepper, the red wine vinegar and the lemon juice, and stir in the parsley. Taste and add more salt and vinegar as necessary (lentils can take quite a bit of both and are vastly improved by them).

Meanwhile, to cook the carrots, first preheat the oven to 190°C, Gas Mark 5. Halve the clementines and put them on a baking tray with the carrots; toss all in the oil. Sprinkle the fennel seeds, salt and pepper over them. Bake for around an hour, turning them a couple of times during cooking, until they are softened and lightly caramelised.

To assemble the dish, make a bed of lentils on a serving dish and top with the carrots and the torn mozzarella. Squeeze over the roasted clementines (and then discard), drizzle over the olive oil, and serve.

Roast rhubarb with amaretti crumble

The forced rhubarb starts to appear early in January, particularly those stems that are harvested by candlelight in traditional sheds in the Yorkshire 'Rhubarb Triangle' (the 23sq km triangle between Leeds, Bradford and Wakefield in West Yorkshire). Look out for it, and when you get hold of some of this precious crop roast it, rather than stewing it, and it will hold its shape and its glorious hot pink colour. You can make the components of this ahead of time and keep the rhubarb in the refrigerator and the crumble in an airtight container for 24 hours, then assemble them at the last moment. Serve topped with a dollop of Greek yoghurt.

Serves 4

Ingredients

10 stems forced rhubarb, sliced into 5cm pieces

4 tablespoons runny honey

Zest and juice of 1 Seville orange

2 star anise

For the crumble topping

80g butter

2 tablespoons runny honey

60g amaretti biscuits, lightly crushed

60g flaked almonds

60g oats

Greek yoghurt, to serve

Method

Preheat the oven to 180°C, Gas Mark 4. Place the rhubarb pieces in a deep-sided baking tray with the honey, orange zest and juice and star anise. Bake for around 20 minutes, or until the rhubarb is tender but still holding its shape.

For the crumble topping, melt the butter and honey in a saucepan and add the crushed amaretti biscuits, almonds and oats. Stir until all is combined, then spread out the mixture on a baking tray and bake alongside the rhubarb for 15–20 minutes or until lightly toasted. Remove from the oven, stir and leave to cool, stirring occasionally.

Serve the crumble scattered over the rhubarb, and eat at room temperature topped with chilled Greek yoghurt.

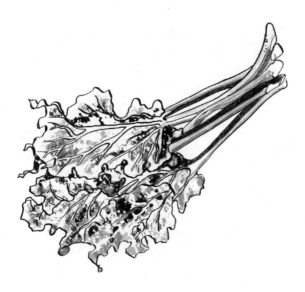

WINTER FISH

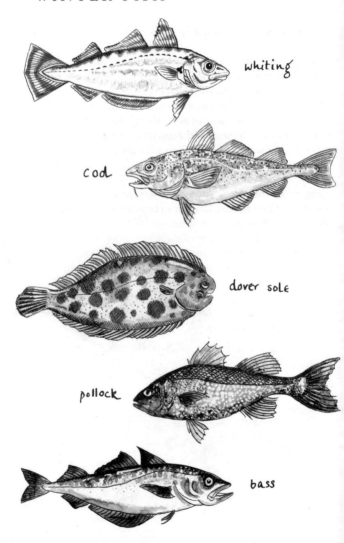

whiting

cod

dover sole

pollock

bass

CHARM OF THE MONTH

Calennig and coal for New Year's Day

Some days are naturally more strongly invested with meaning
than others and so have held particular weight when it comes
to luck and charms, and 1st January is one of them, acting as
a hopeful microcosm for the whole year. Charms have always
lent a sense of control and security where little existed, or
have been used to hold on to the special qualities of certain
moments of the year. On New Year's Day throughout the
British Isles, charms must be carried through doors to carry
in luck for the year ahead. In the southeast of Wales, children
carry from door to door an apple skewered with sticks, cloves
and pieces of evergreens, thought to bring luck and prosperity,
and in return they are given 'calennig' – New Year's gifts of
pennies or sweets. Sometimes the apples are then placed on
windowsills to bring the household good luck through the
year. In Scotland and the north of England, 'first footing'
relates to the first person through your door on New Year's
Day. Ideally it should be a bachelor, and he must have been
out of the house at midnight. He should bring coal, bread,
a coin, a piece of greenery, salt or whisky over the threshold.

A SONG FOR JANUARY'S FULL MOON

'The Fox and the Goose'
Traditional, arr. Richard Barnard

This song follows a wily fox out on a chilly moonlit night. It started life as a 15th-century English poem and then made its way across the Atlantic to become a popular bluegrass song, albeit with a different tune to the original. This is closer to the old English version.

The fox went out on a winter night
And he prayed to the moon to give him light,
For he had no coal or candlelight
To guide him to the town-o...

The false fox came upon a croft
And there he stalked the geese so soft
For he had been here so fearful oft
When he had come to town-o...

He took a goose fast by the neck
And threw it quick behind his back.
The other geese began to quack
But he wouldn't lay it down-o...

The good man came out with his flail
And smote the fox upon the tail,
'Please come no more unto our hall
To bear our geese away-o, way-o, way-o...'

The false fox ran back to his den
And there he was all merry then,
His wife and whelps could eat again
And chew upon the bones-o...

Orion

February

- **1**   Imbolc (pagan/neopagan celebration)

- **1**   Start of LGBT History Month

- **2**   Candlemas (Christian)

- **14**   St Valentine's Day/Birds' Wedding Day

- **15**   Parinirvana Day/Nirvana Day –
  commemorating Buddha's life and
  achievement of parinirvana (Buddhist)

- **25**   Shrove Tuesday – Pancake Day

- **26**   Ash Wednesday – start of Lent
  (Christian)

THE MOON

Names for February's full moon – Snow Moon, Ice Moon, Storm Moon

Even if there is not enough snow to justify the medieval moon name Snow Moon this month, the full moon on the 9th will light up snowy expanses across meadows, woodlands and river banks as snowdrop time reaches its peak. Snowdrops began popping their heads out of the cold ground in January, proving that even though the ground is still bare and hard with frost, spring is straining at the bit. The names Ice Moon and Storm Moon also hint at an understandable preoccupation with this month's weather in the past, when heating meant a few logs on the fire to fend off the deep chill of February. The nights are still long and dark and there are likely to be hard frosts – a wonderful time for spotting constellations if you can stand the cold – but nights are noticeably shortening as spring draws nearer and the days start to lengthen.

Moon phases

1st quarter – *2nd February, 01.42*

Full moon – *9th February, 07.33*

3rd quarter – *15th February, 22.17*

New moon – *23rd February, 15.32*

Moonrise and set

	Lowestoft		Dunquin		
	Rise	Set	Rise	Set	
1st	10.39	–	11.29	00.33	
2nd	10.58	00.51	11.49	01.41	1st quarter
3rd	11.21	02.01	12.12	02.51	
4th	11.50	03.12	12.41	04.02	
5th	12.28	04.22	13.20	05.12	
6th	13.18	05.29	14.11	06.18	
7th	14.23	06.27	15.16	07.15	
8th	15.39	07.14	16.33	08.03	
9th	17.04	07.51	17.57	08.40	full moon
10th	18.32	08.21	19.24	09.09	
11th	19.59	08.45	20.51	09.34	
12th	21.25	09.06	22.16	09.55	
13th	22.49	09.26	23.40	10.16	
14th	–	09.47	–	10.37	
15th	00.11	10.09	01.02	11.00	3rd quarter
16th	01.32	10.36	02.22	11.27	
17th	02.48	11.09	03.38	12.01	
18th	03.58	11.50	04.47	12.42	
19th	04.58	12.40	05.47	13.32	
20th	05.48	13.39	06.36	14.31	
21st	06.26	14.44	07.15	15.36	
22nd	06.57	15.52	07.45	16.44	
23rd	07.21	17.01	08.09	17.53	new moon
24th	07.41	18.09	08.29	19.01	
25th	07.58	19.17	08.47	20.08	
26th	08.13	20.24	09.03	21.15	
27th	08.28	21.31	09.18	22.21	
28th	08.44	22.38	09.34	23.29	
29th	09.02	23.47	09.52	–	

Where moonset times are before moonrise times, this is the setting of the previous night's moon.

Gardening by the moon

New moon to 1st quarter: 1st–2nd and 23rd–29th.
Sow crops that develop below ground. Dig the soil.

1st quarter to full moon: 2nd–9th. Sow crops that develop above ground. Plant seedlings and young plants.

Full moon to 3rd quarter: 9th–15th.
Harvest crops for immediate eating. Harvest fruit.

3rd quarter to new moon: 15th–23rd.
Prune. Harvest for storage. Fertilise and mulch the soil.

February moon dates

9th and 23rd – new moon and full moon: best fishing days.
Some fishermen believe that fish bite best in the 45 minutes either side of moonrise and set on the new and full moons. So that would be 90 minutes from 07.06 and 16.19 on the 9th, and from 06.36 and 16.16 on the 23rd (Lowestoft times).
9th – full moon: Tabodwe. Buddhist full moon festival.
23rd – new moon in Pisces. February's new moon is in intuitive Pisces, so astrologers believe this is a time to allow yourself to follow your instincts. The results will be seen when the full moon is in Pisces on 2nd September.
25th (predicted) – day after the sighting of the new crescent moon: the start of Rajab. Rajab is one of the four sacred months of Islam. The 27th Rajab, Isra and Mi'raj (22nd March this year), celebrates Muhammad's ascent to heaven.
26th – 40 days before the Paschal Moon: Ash Wednesday, the start of Lent. Easter Sunday (12th April this year) falls on the Sunday after the first full moon after the vernal equinox. Lent begins 46 days before that (the six Lent Sundays are not counted in the 40-day abstention period).
26th – day after the calculated first sighting of the new crescent moon: the start of Adar. The spirit of Purim permeates the month – commemorating the deliverance of the Jewish people in ancient Persia from Haman's plot to eliminate all Jews in one day. Purim falls on the 13th and 14th of Adar (9th and 10th of March this year).

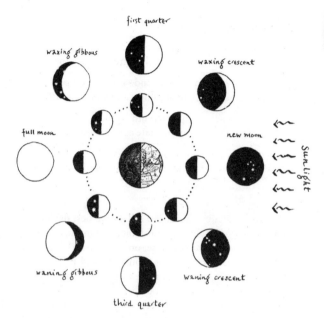

Lunar phases

The moon takes a full month to move around the earth, though obviously it looks like it is moving faster because we keep on spinning around and spotting it again. When we talk about its phases what we are referring to is how much of it is lit by the sun, and this is determined by whether it is between us and the sun, and so we are seeing its dark side, or on the other side of the earth from the sun, in which case we are seeing it fully lit, or at some point in between.

The period when the shape of the moon is growing, between the moon being new and dark and it being full and bright, is called a 'waxing' moon, and the phase when it is thinning, between full and new, is called 'waning'. The shape of the moon when it is less than half full is called a 'crescent' moon and the shape when it is more than half full is a 'gibbous' moon.

THE SKY

At night

27th Look out for a close approach of the moon and
Venus visible in the southwestern dusk from about 17.30,
at an altitude of 35 degrees. They will set at about 21.00
in the west.

By day

The sun reaches an altitude of 28 degrees in the London
sky and 24 degrees in the Glasgow sky at midday on 21st
February.

Day length increases by 1h 48m in Lowestoft, Suffolk, and
by 1h 46m in Dunquin, Republic of Ireland.

Earliest sunrise: 29th February, Lowestoft 06.40, Dunquin
07.29.

Latest sunset: 29th February, Lowestoft 17.30, Dunquin
18.20.

Sunrise and set

	Lowestoft		*Dunquin*	
	Rise	Set	Rise	Set
1st	07.35	16.38	08.23	17.28
2nd	07.33	16.40	08.21	17.30
3rd	07.32	16.41	08.19	17.31
4th	07.30	16.43	08.18	17.33
5th	07.28	16.45	08.16	17.35
6th	07.27	16.47	08.14	17.37
7th	07.25	16.49	08.13	17.39
8th	07.23	16.51	08.11	17.41
9th	07.21	16.53	08.09	17.43
10th	07.19	16.55	08.07	17.45
11th	07.18	16.57	08.05	17.46
12th	07.16	16.59	08.03	17.48
13th	07.14	17.00	08.02	17.50
14th	07.12	17.02	08.00	17.52
15th	07.10	17.04	07.58	17.54
16th	07.08	17.06	07.56	17.56
17th	07.06	17.08	07.54	17.58
18th	07.04	17.10	07.52	18.00
19th	07.02	17.12	07.50	18.01
20th	07.00	17.14	07.48	18.03
21st	06.58	17.16	07.46	18.05
22nd	06.55	17.17	07.44	18.07
23rd	06.53	17.19	07.41	18.09
24th	06.51	17.21	07.39	18.11
25th	06.49	17.23	07.37	18.13
26th	06.47	17.25	07.35	18.14
27th	06.45	17.27	07.33	18.16
28th	06.43	17.29	07.31	18.18
29th	06.40	17.30	07.29	18.20

THE SEA

Average sea temperature

Ayr:	7.7°C
Sunderland:	6.9°C
Dingle:	10.1°C
Dublin:	8.8°C
Aberystwyth:	8.5°C
Lowestoft:	7.0°C
Poole:	9.2°C
Newquay:	10.0°C

Spring and neap tides

The spring tides are the most extreme tides of the month, with the highest rises and falls, and the neap tides are the least extreme, with the smallest. Exact timings vary around the coast, but expect them around the following dates:

Spring tides: 11th–12th and 25th–26th

Neap tides: 3rd–4th and 17th–18th

In the tide timetable opposite, spring tides are shown with an asterisk.

February tide timetable for Dover

For guidance on how to convert this for your local area, see page 8.

| | High water | | Low water | |
	Morning	Afternoon	Morning	Afternoon
1st	03.00	15.22	10.23	22.36
2nd	03.44	16.15	11.08	23.27
3rd	04.46	17.49	–	12.11
4th	06.15	19.10	00.42	13.35
5th	07.30	20.11	02.10	14.49
6th	08.30	21.04	03.19	15.51
7th	09.23	21.52	04.18	16.48
8th	10.11	22.37	05.13	17.42
9th	10.57	23.21	06.06	18.34
10th	11.41	–	06.57	19.23
11th*	00.04	12.24	07.46	20.07
12th*	00.48	13.08	08.31	20.47
13th	01.32	13.53	09.12	21.26
14th	02.18	14.41	09.53	22.05
15th	03.07	15.33	10.35	22.49
16th	04.01	16.34	11.23	23.43
17th	05.05	17.49	–	12.23
18th	06.24	19.15	00.51	13.33
19th	07.57	20.35	02.08	14.50
20th	09.15	21.35	03.32	16.18
21st	10.08	22.20	04.50	17.22
22nd	10.49	22.58	05.44	18.07
23rd	11.23	23.33	06.27	18.44
24th	11.54	–	07.03	19.15
25th*	00.07	12.24	07.32	19.39
26th*	00.39	12.53	07.57	20.01
27th	01.06	13.17	08.20	20.26
28th	01.26	13.37	08.46	20.54
29th	01.48	14.01	09.15	21.26

NATURE

The hedgerow in February

Along the base of the hedgerow comes a smattering of hopeful yellow and white this month: lesser celandine, winter aconite, primroses and snowdrops appear, and there will also be a few purple dog violets in the mix if you're lucky. Wood anemones start into flower this month. They are an indicator species for ancient woodland so if you spot them you know that you are dealing with a remnant of a very old piece of woodland indeed, possibly a thousand years old or more. On the warm days this month it can suddenly feel like spring is here: the first butterflies – pale yellow-green brimstones – emerge and flit about the flowers in the weak sun, having overwintered in nooks and crannies in the hedge. Queen buff-tailed and early bumblebees emerge from the holes in the ground where they have spent the winter, and visit flowers to drink nectar and strengthen up after winter. Each queen searches for an underground nest site under tussocky grass, and when she has chosen one, she visits the hazel catkins to collect pollen. Back in the nest she mixes the pollen with wax from her body and lays her first brood onto it.

A few of the blackberries of the wild privet bushes cling on, but this is a lean time for foraging, and so most creatures are still conserving their energies, sleeping or hibernating. Deer may creep along the hedge line using it for shelter, protection and grazing. It is time for a spring-clean in the badger setts below the hedge, with the badgers pulling out the old winter bedding and dragging in fresh beds of dried bracken and leaves.

FROGS/FROGSPAWN

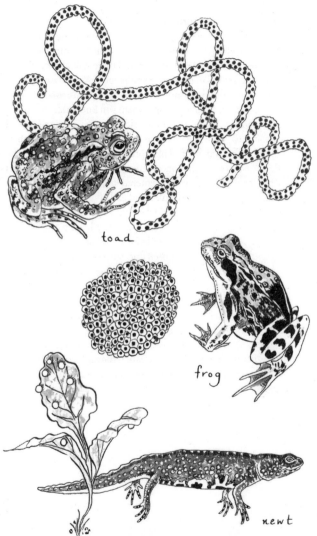

toad

frog

newt

THE FLOWER GARDEN

February's flower garden picking prompts

A little jam jar of whatever early spring bulbs you have –
aconites, crocuses and narcissus with a sprig of rosemary;
a glass of snowdrops for Candlemas on 2nd February
(it is unlucky to bring them into the house any other day,
but take your chances as you will…); a single branch
of flowering camellia in a narrow-necked vase.

Jobs in the flower garden

- Choose and order dahlia tubers now, as the best sell out
  early. You might go for a delicate peachy combination of
  'Café au Lait', 'Jowey Linda' and 'Nicholas'; a pinky-
  purple mixture of 'Orfeo', 'Pink Magic' and 'Trustful';
  or many, many other combinations. Pick a colour scheme
  and go crazy.
- Clematis that flower at the height of summer or after
  should be pruned now (spring ones should be left until
  after flowering). Don't cut them too close to the ground,
  as the shoots are loved by slugs – leave a clearance of
  30cm or so and consider putting in place some slug
  protection, such as copper slug rings.
- You will need to get your lilies into pots this month or
  next. Either plant into terracotta pots for flanking a
  doorway or path, or put them in plastic pots that you can
  sink into your border when their flowering time is nigh.
  Lilium regale has white trumpet flowers flushed with pink
  and will waft the most incredible spicy scent around your
  garden on summer evenings.

THE KITCHEN GARDEN

Plan spring's sowings and put in your main seed order now, as the best varieties will sell out. Buy and chit potatoes (see page 22) if you didn't last month. Clear and prepare soil for planting out, and put cloches, or clear or black plastic, over beds to warm soil for early sowings. Start tomatoes and aubergines towards the end of the month, once the chilli seeds have germinated and have been moved out of the heated propagator. Plant out garlic and shallot sets if it is not too wet. Cut autumn raspberry canes down to the ground. Hand pollinate peaches and nectarines using a soft brush, and protect them from rain if you can, to prevent peach leaf curl.

Sowing and planting crops

Fruit/veg	Sow under cover	Sow direct	Plant
Chillies	✓*		
Aubergines	✓*		
Sweet peppers	✓*		
Brussels sprouts	✓		
Globe artichokes	✓		
Kohlrabi	✓		
Leeks	✓		
Lettuces	✓		
Onions	✓		
Peas	✓		
Radishes	✓		
Salad leaves	✓		
Spinach	✓		
Sprouting broccoli	✓		
Broad beans	✓		
Garlic			✓
Shallot sets			✓
Fruit trees/bushes			✓

*In heated propagator

THE KITCHEN

Sauce of the month – vinaigrette

Now that winter lettuces and salad leaves are starting to grow again in the garden, it is time to perfect your vinaigrette. The usual recommendation is three parts oil to one part acid – vinegar or citrus juice – but this can be overwhelmingly acidic, so try four or five parts oil to one part acid, and then add more vinegar or citrus juice if you need it. Put all into a jar along with salt and pepper, a pinch of sugar and a few additions if you like, then shake to combine. Some possible combinations: honey, mustard and finely chopped rosemary; chopped tarragon with lemon zest and lemon juice; a little sesame oil instead of olive oil, plus soy sauce and grated ginger; crushed garlic and anchovy; orange zest and juice with thyme; rice wine vinegar and lime juice with lime zest and chilli flakes.

In season

Vegetables: wild garlic, kale, winter cauliflowers, chard, perpetual spinach, leeks, cabbages, celeriac, parsnips, swede, purple sprouting broccoli, Brussels sprouts, winter lettuces, salad leaves, endive
Herbs: winter savory, parsley, chervil, coriander, rosemary, bay, sage
Fruit: imported blood oranges and kiwi fruits, forced rhubarb, stored apples and pears
Wild meat: last month of the venison season
Fish: clams, cockles and mussels, lemon sole, bass, bream, cod, whiting, haddock

RECIPES

Htamanè – full moon festival sticky rice
A recipe by MiMi Aye

The 9th February is the full moon day of Tabodwe – roughly equivalent to February – on the Burmese lunar calendar, and the traditional food of the day in Myanmar is the savoury delicacy *htamanè*. A giant wok is set up on a low stove and the ingredients are pounded together by three strong men of the village. They use massive oar-like spatulas while chanting and singing shanties, and everyone sings, dances and claps along with them. Once the *htamanè* is pounded to a paste, it is finished with fried coconut slices, salted peanuts and sesame seeds. A dish is set aside to be presented to the Buddha before the rest is distributed among friends and family as a moon festival gift. In the UK, a few Buddhist monasteries such as the Tisarana Vihara in London keep up the tradition for the local Burmese community, although it tends to be one wok rather than ten woks in play. The following recipe is a domestic version which lacks some of the grandeur of a traditional *htamanè*, but tastes just as good. Serve with cups of green tea.

Serves 4–6
Ingredients
25g black glutinous rice
475g white glutinous rice
200ml oil
100g fresh coconut, cut into 3mm x 3cm slices
40g shredded ginger
1 tablespoon salt
175g salted peanuts
4 tablespoons sesame seeds

Method

Soak the black rice overnight in 300ml warm water. The next day, soak the white rice for 2 hours in 350ml warm water.

Heat the oil in a wok over medium-high heat, and fry half the coconut slices for 2–3 minutes till slightly toasted. Drain them on kitchen paper and set to one side. Pour out half of the oil from the wok into a heatproof bowl and set to one side.

Add the shredded ginger to the wok and fry for 2–3 minutes until fragrant and then add both types of rice, the water you soaked them in, the salt and 200ml water. Mix well and cover. Bring to the boil, stir and cover again. Lower the heat and simmer for 20 minutes.

Add the reserved oil and 100ml water, stirring over a low heat until the water is absorbed. Add the unfried coconut slices, peanuts and 3 tablespoons of the sesame seeds; mix through. Now use 2 spatulas to stir and knead everything together over a low heat for 15–20 minutes till the cooked rice breaks down and becomes smooth.

Sprinkle the remaining tablespoon of sesame seeds and the fried coconut slices over the top. Serve while it's still warm.

Pear, apple and rosemary fritters for Fritter Thursday

Each day of the first week of Lent has a name – Collop
Monday, Shrove Tuesday, Ash Wednesday, Fritter Thursday
and Kissing Friday. On Fritter Thursday it was traditional to
eat apple fritters: pieces of apple dipped into batter and fried.
This recipe mixes apples, pears and a little finely chopped
rosemary to make sweet, crunchy and herby fritters, which
are delicious with vanilla ice cream.

Makes about 15 fritters
Ingredients
Vegetable or sunflower oil for deep frying
Zest and juice of 1 lemon
2 apples
2 pears
½ teaspoon fresh rosemary, finely chopped
1 tablespoon caster sugar
3 tablespoons plain flour
Pinch of salt

Method

Fill a deep pan no more than a third full of oil and place on
the heat.

Put the lemon juice in a bowl, then peel the apples and
pears and grate them into it, tossing the grated fruit in the
lemon juice to prevent discolouring. Tip the grated fruit into
the centre of a clean tea towel. Gather up the tea towel, holding
the corners together around the ball of apple and pear. Squeeze
out the moisture into the sink.

Put the fruit in a clean bowl and break it apart with a fork, then add the lemon zest, rosemary, sugar, flour and salt, and use the fork to mix everything together so the fruit is well coated.

Check that the oil is hot by dropping a small cube of bread in it. If it starts to fizzle immediately and turns brown within 60 seconds, the oil is the right temperature – if it browns much faster than this, allow the oil to cool a little.

Shape the mixture in little balls, using two teaspoons for each. Lower five or six carefully into the oil, and fry for a minute or two until they are toasty brown all over. Drain the cooked fritters on kitchen paper and keep them warm in a low oven. Fry the remainder in the same way. Serve hot with vanilla ice cream.

CHARM OF THE MONTH

A red petticoat for leap day proposals

This is a leap year, and so we have a rare 29th February on our hands. There are lots of traditions surrounding leap days, but chief among them is the convention that it was the day women could propose to men. St Brigid – whose saint day falls at the beginning of this month – is said to have brought this about, haggling with St Patrick to balance men's and women's traditional roles. Getting to propose on one day in four years was apparently deemed sufficient…If you are going to propose on the 29th, a red petticoat is thought to bring more luck in the endeavour, if you flash it at your suitor before proposing, though some other red undergarment might have similarly persuasive powers if you don't have a petticoat to hand. This practice may originate from women traditionally dying their petticoats to indicate they were betrothed, which would make it something of a *fait accomplis*. Certainly, refusing a woman on this day was strongly frowned upon, and there used to be laws forbidding it, though these were later softened to a law stating that any man refusing a woman's leap day proposal must buy her a pair of gloves at Easter – perhaps it was to disguise her unmarried state.

A SONG FOR FEBRUARY'S FULL MOON

'The Moon Shined on My Bed Last Night'
Traditional, arr. Richard Barnard

This beautiful Scottish ballad finds a young woman lamenting marrying for money. In some versions she sets out to find her true love, and hang the consequences. Alas, in this one she simply languishes in the moonlight, broken-hearted.

The moon shone on my bed last night,
No rest there could I find
For thinking of that bonnie boy,
The boy I left behind.
If he were here that I love dear
I'd sleep here in my bed,
But instead of sleep all night I weep
And mony's the tear I shed.

For an auld man came a-courting me
He sought me for his bride.
My parents they advised me so
To have him by my side.
He had a little money,
It was all they would endure,
But I'd rather go a-roving
With my roving bonnie boy.

For some speak ill of my true love
And mony speak ill of me,
But I let them all say whit they will
I'd rather his company.
If he were here that I love dear
I'd sleep here in my bed,
But instead of sleep all night I weep
And mony's the tear I shed.

March

- **1** Start of meteorological spring
- **1** St David's Day – patron saint of Wales
- **5** St Piran's Day – patron saint of Cornwall
- **9** Commonwealth Day
- **9** Holi (Hindu spring festival)
- **9** 9th/10th: Purim (Jewish celebration)
- **9** Mucenici/Little Saints (Romanian tradition)
- **17** St Patrick's Day – patron saint of Ireland – bank holiday, Northern Ireland and Republic of Ireland
- **20** Vernal equinox – start of astronomical spring
- **20** Ostara (neopagan celebration of spring)
- **20** Nowruz (Iranian/Persian New Year)
- **22** Fourth Sunday in Lent – Mothering Sunday
- **25** Lady Day, The Feast of the Annunciation (Christian)
- **29** British Summer Time (BST) and Irish Standard Time (IST) begin – both are Universal Coordinated Time (UTC) + 1 hour. Clocks go forward one hour at 01.00

THE MOON

Names for March's full moon – Plough Moon, Wind Moon, Lenten Moon, Chaste Moon

Finally spring feels unstoppable and the landscape beneath this month's full moon on the 9th is easing its way out of winter's grip, with banks of pale wild daffodils swaying in the March breezes and dots of blossom visible under its silvery light. Throughout the year we will see a series of moon names that reference big seasonal jobs, and the Plough Moon is the first of these, perhaps suggesting that the light of the full moon allowed people to carry on ploughing well into the evening. Farming and gardening begin in earnest this month, often in gusty conditions, as the name Wind Moon suggests.

The name Lenten Moon for March's full moon on the 9th partially reflects the fact that we are now mid-Lent, and the Celtic name Chaste Moon may also allude to Lent's constraints. But the word itself originates in the Old English word *lencten*, which means 'spring' and is in reference to the lengthening days, which are hard to ignore as this month we reach the equinox, when day and night are finally the same length.

Moon phases

1st quarter – *2nd March, 19.57*

Full moon – *9th March, 17.48*

3rd quarter – *16th March, 09.34*

New moon – *24th March, 09.28*

Moonrise and set

	Lowestoft		*Dunquin*		
	Rise	Set	Rise	Set	
1st	09.22	–	10.13	00.37	
2nd	09.47	00.56	10.39	01.46	1st quarter
3rd	10.20	02.06	11.12	02.55	
4th	11.03	03.12	11.56	04.02	
5th	11.59	04.13	12.52	05.02	
6th	13.09	05.04	14.02	05.52	
7th	14.29	05.45	15.22	06.33	
8th	15.56	06.17	16.49	07.06	
9th	17.25	06.44	18.18	07.33	full moon
10th	18.54	07.07	19.46	07.56	
11th	20.23	07.27	21.14	08.17	
12th	21.50	07.48	22.41	08.38	
13th	23.15	08.10	–	09.01	
14th	–	08.36	00.05	09.27	
15th	00.36	09.07	01.26	09.59	
16th	01.50	09.46	02.40	10.38	3rd quarter
17th	02.55	10.34	03.44	11.27	
18th	03.48	11.31	04.36	12.24	
19th	04.30	12.35	05.18	13.28	
20th	05.02	13.42	05.50	14.35	
21st	05.27	14.51	06.15	15.43	
22nd	05.47	15.59	06.36	16.51	
23rd	06.05	17.07	06.54	17.59	
24th	06.20	18.14	07.09	19.05	new moon
25th	06.35	19.21	07.25	20.12	
26th	06.50	20.29	07.40	21.20	
27th	07.07	21.37	07.57	22.28	
28th	07.26	22.47	08.16	23.37	
29th	08.49	–	09.40	-	
30th	09.18	00.56	10.09	01.45	
31st	09.59	02.03	10.48	02.52	

British Summer Time and Irish Standard Time begin on 29th March at 01.00, and this is accounted for above.
Where moonset times are before moonrise times, this is the setting of the previous night's moon.

Gardening by the moon

New moon to 1st quarter: 1st–2nd and 24th–31st.
Sow crops that develop below ground. Dig the soil.

1st quarter to full moon: 2nd–9th. Sow crops that develop above ground. Plant seedlings and young plants.

Full moon to 3rd quarter: 9th–16th.
Harvest crops for immediate eating. Harvest fruit.

3rd quarter to new moon: 16th–24th.
Prune. Harvest for storage. Fertilise and mulch the soil.

March moon dates

9th – full moon: Magha Puja Day. This is the second-holiest celebration in the Buddhist year, and commemorates a gathering of Buddha and his disciples.
9th and 24th – full moon and new moon: best fishing days. Some fishermen believe that fish bite best in the 45 minutes either side of moonrise and set on the full and new moons. So that would be 90 minutes from 05.59 and 16.40 on the 9th, and from 05.35 and 17.29 on the 24th (Lowestoft times).
9th and 10th – day of and day after full moon: Holi. The Hindu festival of Holi is celebrated the day after the full moon of the month of Phalgun in the Bengali and Nepali calendar.
24th – new moon in Aries. This month's new moon is in the creative and energetic Aries – astrologers believe this is one of the best moments for new projects. You will see the fruits of this the next time the new moon is in Aries, on 1st October.
26th – day after the calculated first sighting of the new crescent moon: the start of Nisan. 'The month of happiness' is the first month of the ecclesiastical Hebrew year and the seventh of the civil calendar. It begins at the sighting of the new crescent moon. Passover begins at twilight on the 14th day of Nisan.
26th (predicted) – day after the sighting of the new crescent moon: the start of Sha'ban. The 15th of the Islamic month of Sha'ban (9th April this year) is Bara'a Night, when sins are forgiven and fortunes are decided for the year ahead.

After Robin Heath, from *Sun, Moon & Earth* (Wooden Books)

When can I see the moon?

When the moon is new it is not only dark – that is, unlit by the sun – but it also rises and sets with the sun and is in the same part of the sky, and so is impossible to see. The crescent of the new moon appears a couple of days later, when the moon pulls a little to the left of the sun, and can be seen briefly after sunset before it follows the sun below the horizon. It then stretches away to the left, day by day, rising and setting progressively later than the sun until finally, at full moon, it is fully nocturnal, rising roughly as the sun sets and setting as the sun rises – acting as its shining mirror. After full moon it changes from setting after the sun to rising before the sun, getting closer to the sun each day until it falls into step and vanishes again, to become a new moon once again.

THE SKY

At night

9th Supermoon. The moon is 357,399km from the earth and almost at its closest point to earth this year (see April for the biggest moon of the year), and so will appear larger and brighter than usual.

18th Close approach of the moon, Jupiter, Saturn and Mars, all visible low above the southeastern horizon from 04.30 until they are lost in the dawn at 06.00.

28th Close approach of the moon and Venus, visible in the western dusk at an altitude of 37 degrees from about 18.30 until setting at 22.30.

By day

The vernal, or spring, equinox falls on 20th March at 03.50. The equinox is the moment at which the centre of the sun is directly above the equator, and so day and night are of equal length all around the globe. (The word comes from the Latin *aequi*, or 'equal', and *nox*, or 'night'.) It occurs twice a year, in March and September.

The sun reaches an altitude of 38 degrees in the London sky and 34 degrees in the Glasgow sky at midday on the vernal equinox on 20th March.

Day length increases by 2h 3m in Lowestoft, Suffolk, and by 2h 1m in Dunquin, Republic of Ireland.

Earliest sunrise: 31st March, Lowestoft 06.28, Dunquin 07.18.

Latest sunset: 31st March, Lowestoft 19.26, Dunquin 20.14.

Sunrise and set

	Lowestoft		Dunquin	
	Rise	Set	Rise	Set
1st	06.38	17.32	07.26	18.22
2nd	06.36	17.34	07.24	18.23
3rd	06.34	17.36	07.22	18.25
4th	06.31	17.38	07.20	18.27
5th	06.29	17.40	07.17	18.29
6th	06.27	17.41	07.15	18.31
7th	06.25	17.43	07.13	18.32
8th	06.22	17.45	07.11	18.34
9th	06.20	17.47	07.08	18.36
10th	06.18	17.49	07.06	18.38
11th	06.15	17.50	07.04	18.40
12th	06.13	17.52	07.02	18.41
13th	06.11	17.54	06.59	18.43
14th	06.08	17.56	06.57	18.45
15th	06.06	17.58	06.55	18.47
16th	06.04	17.59	06.52	18.48
17th	06.01	18.01	06.50	18.50
18th	05.59	18.03	06.48	18.52
19th	05.57	18.05	06.45	18.54
20th	05.54	18.06	06.43	18.55
21st	05.52	18.08	06.41	18.57
22nd	05.50	18.10	06.38	18.59
23rd	05.57	18.12	06.36	19.00
24th	05.45	18.13	06.34	19.02
25th	05.43	18.15	06.31	19.04
26th	05.40	18.17	06.29	19.06
27th	05.38	18.19	06.27	19.07
28th	05.35	18.21	06.24	19.09
29th	06.33	19.22	07.22	20.11
30th	06.31	19.24	07.20	20.13
31st	06.28	19.26	07.18	20.14

British Summer Time and Irish Standard Time begin on 29th March at 01.00, and this is accounted for above.

THE SEA

Average sea temperature

Ayr:	7.7°C
Sunderland:	6.7°C
Dingle:	9.9°C
Dublin:	8.4°C
Aberystwyth:	8.3°C
Lowestoft:	6.8°C
Poole:	8.8°C
Newquay:	9.7°C

Spring and neap tides

The spring tides are the most extreme tides of the month, with the highest rises and falls, and the neap tides are the least extreme, with the smallest. Exact timings vary around the coast, but expect them around the following dates:

Spring tides: 12th–13th and 26th–27th

Neap tides: 4th–5th and 18th–19th

In the tide timetable opposite, spring tides are shown with an asterisk.

March tide timetable for Dover

For guidance on how to convert this for your local area, see page 8.

| | High water | | Low water | |
	Morning	Afternoon	Morning	Afternoon
1st	02.18	14.35	09.47	22.00
2nd	02.57	15.18	10.24	22.43
3rd	03.47	16.18	11.14	23.42
4th	05.05	18.31	–	12.34
5th	07.04	19.47	01.23	14.15
6th	08.13	20.46	02.49	15.26
7th	09.09	21.36	03.54	16.28
8th	09.59	22.22	04.54	17.26
9th	10.44	23.06	05.51	18.21
10th	11.27	23.48	06.45	19.09
11th	–	12.09	07.33	19.52
12th*	00.30	12.50	08.16	20.30
13th*	01.13	13.33	08.54	21.06
14th	01.56	14.18	09.31	21.43
15th	02.43	15.07	10.10	22.24
16th	03.34	16.04	10.55	23.15
17th	04.35	17.14	11.53	–
18th	05.52	18.40	00.24	13.07
19th	07.46	20.15	01.47	14.29
20th	09.07	21.17	03.17	15.59
21st	09.55	22.01	04.35	17.01
22nd	10.32	22.38	05.26	17.45
23rd	11.03	23.11	07.07	18.20
24th	11.31	23.43	06.40	18.48
25th	11.58	–	07.05	19.10
26th*	00.11	12.25	07.27	19.33
27th*	00.35	12.46	07.52	20.00
28th	00.53	13.04	08.19	20.29
29th	01.16	13.30	08.47	20.59
30th	01.46	14.05	09.17	21.33
31st	02.25	14.48	09.54	22.14

NATURE

The hedgerow in March

The hedgerow starts to wake up this month. Muntjac deer may browse and nibble on the new green hedge growth and the lemony sorrel at the base. Pussy willow catkins burst open and clouds of blackthorn blossom appear, its flowers white with long yellow stamens against the still-bare spiky black stems. Peacock, small tortoiseshell and comma butterflies emerge and feed on the pollen, along with queen white-tailed bumblebees, just out of hibernation. Hedgehogs are also waking up to snuffle between the clumps of wild daffodils, searching for slugs on which to fatten themselves up. The spring usher, the early moth and the March moth might be seen in the evenings, and bats – which have been in a state of dormancy all winter and have now reached the end of their fat reserves – start to make short, flitting flights around the hedgerows in search of the moths.

New life is emerging as the weather is at its most unpredictable, and the shelter the hedgerow provides is crucial. For many birds this is nest-building time. Female blackbirds build their sturdy nests low in the hedgerow, while female robins build a dome-shaped nest from grass, leaves and moss on which they lay their first batch of pale, speckled eggs. Wrens do things a little differently: the male builds a succession of nests and invites the female to choose one, which she then lines with feathers. Pairs of song thrushes build their nests together from dry grass and leaves, lining the insides with mud. Linnets are building their nests, too, cup-shaped and lined with moss and feathers. Grey partridges scrape indentations in the ground at the base of the hedgerow and line it with leaves and grasses ready to hold their precious eggs.

SPRING HEDGEROW FLOWERS

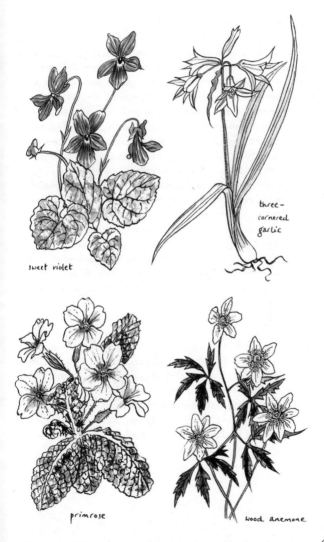

sweet violet

three-cornered garlic

primrose

wood anemone

M

CHARM OF THE MONTH

Four-leaf clover

The association of four-leaf clovers with luck may have arisen from their relative scarcity: only about one in five thousand clovers will have the extra leaf, so those with the extra one are a bit special and worth tucking into your pocket when you need luck on your side. It is said that you will only find one when you're not looking (though once you have, keep looking: the same plant is likely to produce more). They were carried by Welsh Celts as a charm against evil spirits, and there are records of them being used all over the British Isles. However, they are most associated with Ireland and with St Patrick, whose day falls on 17th March, because he is alleged to have taught the Irish the concept of the Holy Trinity using the three-leaved version. When they are not representing the Father, the Son and the Holy Ghost, the three leaves represent faith, hope and love, with the exceptional fourth adding luck. It is said that there are more four-leaf clovers in Ireland than there are in the rest of the British Isles, thus accounting for the 'luck of the Irish'.

THE FLOWER GARDEN

March's flower garden picking prompts
A froth of blossom; a cheery bunch of daffs with wallflowers; a single, kinked stem of magnolia in a narrow vase.

Jobs in the flower garden

- Under glass, sow your hardy annuals for picking this month: *Ammi majus*, calendula, larkspur, sunflowers, love-in-a-mist, California poppy, scabious, opium poppy, dill and quaking grass. Sow them into modules for easy potting on or planting out.

- Buy and plant lily of the valley 'pips' – shoots and roots ready to grow and flower. They have gone out of fashion now but were once routinely forced for early flowers by being grown indoors. Plant them in a pot and place them outside or in a greenhouse for fragrant flowers in May.

- Plant a few florist's chrysanthemums for cutting and to guarantee autumnal cut flowers after all else has faded. Buy plug plants now and pot them on, then plant them out when frosts have passed. They will start into flower in September and can keep going all the way to December.

THE KITCHEN GARDEN

Courgettes, winter squash and tomatoes should be started in
a heated propagator but not until halfway through the month:
any sooner and they will grow leggy and weak before it is warm
enough to plant them out. This month you can start to make
sowings direct outdoors if the weather is mild, but do so on
areas where you have warmed the soil with cloches or by laying
down black or clear plastic sheeting. Apply an organic high-
potash fertiliser around your fruit trees and bushes and mulch
them with garden compost or well-rotted farmyard manure.
Keep pollinating peach and nectarine blossom with a soft
paintbrush. Prepare soil for more direct sowing next month.

Sowing and planting crops

Fruit/veg	Sow under cover	Sow direct	Plant
Tomatoes	✔*		
Courgettes	✔*		
Cucumbers	✔*		
Aubergines	✔*		
Winter squash	✔*		
Pumpkins	✔*		
Chillies	✔*		
Sweet peppers	✔*		
Globe artichokes	✔		
Lettuces	✔		
Spinach	✔		✔
Salad leaves	✔		
Spring onions		✔	
Coriander	✔		
Parsley	✔		
Chervil	✔		
Dill	✔		
Florence fennel	✔		
Summer cabbages	✔		

Fruit/veg	Sow under cover	Sow direct	Plant
Autumn cabbages	✓		
Parsnips		✓	
Peas		✓	✓
Leeks		✓	
Turnips	✓	✓	
Rocket	✓	✓	
Beetroot	✓	✓	
Carrots	✓	✓	
Summer cauliflowers		✓	✓
Sprouting broccoli	✓		
Calabrese		✓	
Broad beans		✓	✓
Early potatoes			✓
Onion and shallot sets			✓
Garlic			✓
Asparagus			✓
Rhubarb			✓
Strawberries			✓
Raspberries			✓
Blackberries			✓
Apples and pears			✓
Gooseberries			✓
Currants			✓

*In heated propagator

THE KITCHEN

Sauce of the month – garlicky green goddess dressing

Green goddess dressing was popular in the 1970s and 1980s but fell out of favour for who knows what reason. It is herby and piquant and it looks beautiful, with its creamy pale green colour. The version given here uses this month's woodland wild garlic bounty, but at other times of year you can revert to the retro greenery of parsley, tarragon and chives. The most important thing is that you use a food processor or blender to whizz the ingredients together and make a smooth sauce. We want nothing rustic and chunky here. Put about 30 washed and dried wild garlic leaves into the food processor with 300ml soured cream, the juice of half a lemon, and salt and pepper. Blitz until smooth, and serve immediately drizzled over green salads or used as a dipping sauce for crudités and hunks of bread. It is best used straight away because the fresh, mild garlic flavour intensifies to 'a bit too garlicky actually, thanks' after just a few hours. If making this with herbs instead of wild garlic, you might add a couple of anchovies and a clove of crushed garlic, but the wild garlic needs no such help.

In season

Vegetables: wild garlic, sorrel, kale, winter cauliflowers, chard, perpetual spinach, leeks, cabbages, parsnips, purple sprouting broccoli, spring onions, winter lettuces, Brussels sprouts, spring cabbages, chicory

Herbs: winter savory, parsley, chervil, coriander, rosemary, bay, sage

Fruit: forced rhubarb, stored cooking apples

Fish: oysters, mussels, coley, dab, lemon sole, cod, haddock, whiting, pollock

RECIPES

Sorrel, sprouting broccoli and egg pizza

Once you get into the habit of making pizzas, you can use them as a base for a host of seasonal ingredients. This one uses a very simple mascarpone and Parmesan white sauce as the base instead of a tomato sauce, and is all the more fresh and springy for it. This will make four meal-sized pizzas but you can just make one and freeze the dough in portions for another time if you quarter the topping ingredients. If you have a pizza stone or a pizza oven, you may be able to shorten the process by putting the toppings on without prebaking the base, but pizzas are tricky to cook through in conventional ovens unless you do it as instructed here.

Makes 4 pizzas

Ingredients

For the bases

500g strong white flour, plus extra for dusting

2 teaspoons salt

1 teaspoon instant dried yeast

1 tablespoon extra virgin olive oil

325ml warm water

For the toppings

100g piece of Parmesan

150g mascarpone

1 ½ tablespoons extra virgin olive oil

A few sorrel leaves, sliced crossways into ribbons

12 small spears purple sprouting broccoli, lightly steamed

4 large eggs

2 tablespoons of olive oil

Salt and pepper

Method

Measure the flour, salt, yeast, olive oil and warm water into a large bowl. Mix with your hands until well combined and then tip out onto a floured surface and knead for 10 minutes. Place the dough in a clean bowl, cover with a tea towel, and leave to rise in a warm place for 2 hours or until it has doubled in size.

Meanwhile, grate half the Parmesan and thinly slice the other half, then break it into little chunks. Put the mascarpone into a bowl, and mix in the Parmesan, olive oil, ¼ teaspoon of salt and a few grinds of pepper. When all is nicely combined, stir in the sorrel leaves.

Preheat the oven to 240°C, Gas Mark 9. Tip the risen dough out onto a floured surface and divide it into four equal pieces. Roll one piece out to dinner-plate size (or an oval equivalent, depending on your baking tray), place it on a floured baking tray and put it into the oven for 6 minutes.

Remove the half-cooked pizza base from the oven and spread a quarter of the cheese mixture over the base. Top with 3 broccoli spears, and crack an egg into the centre. Add a drizzle of olive oil and a little salt and pepper, and return to the oven for 7 minutes or until the egg white is cooked. Repeat with the other three pieces of dough. Serve hot.

Romanian *mucenici*/little saints for Mucenici on 9th March
By Irina Georgescu

There is a large Romanian population in the British Isles, and each year, on 9th March, Romanians celebrate Mucenici. This religious culinary tradition sees everybody eating little doughs simmered in a rum-spiked walnut and vanilla soup. The figure-of-eight shape of the *mucenici* is related to the symbol for infinity and to the cyclic rhythm of life and of seasons. Mucenici is a religious tradition remembering 40 people who were sentenced to death by a Roman legion for their Christian beliefs. They were left to drown in a freezing lake, but they didn't die. This miracle itself convinced some Roman soldiers to convert to the new religion. The following day, having been found alive, the Christians were tortured to their deaths, but they were immediately recognised as martyrs by their followers, and have been celebrated ever since. In the Romanian agricultural calendar, Mucenici marks a transitional 40-day period from the last aggressive impulses of winter with its frosty blasts, to the warm, sunny moods of spring. We like to celebrate it with 40 shots of *țuică* – Romanian plum brandy – and with a bowl full of *mucenici*.

Makes 40–45 *mucenici*, to serve 4 people

Ingredients

For the dough

90ml hot water

150g plain flour

Pinch of salt

For cooking

700ml water

4 tablespoons sugar

25g honey

125g walnuts, roughly chopped

Zest of 1 lemon and 2 oranges

4 teaspoons vanilla essence

25ml rum

2 teaspoons cinnamon

Method

To make the dough, add the hot water to the flour and salt, and stir well until it reaches room temperature. Knead the dough briefly and divide into 40–45 balls, each 5–7g in weight. Roll each ball into a 10cm-long rope, join the ends to form a circle, and then twist in the middle to create a figure-of-eight. Place all the shapes on a baking tray, and either allow to dry overnight or dry in an oven at 110°C, Gas Mark ¼ for 2 hours.

Bring the water, sugar and honey to a boil. Reduce the heat to medium, add the little dough shapes and simmer for 10 minutes. Add the walnuts and citrus zest, cooking for a further 5 minutes. Remove the pan from the heat and add the vanilla, rum and cinnamon. Allow to cool for a few minutes, then serve.

A SONG FOR MARCH'S FULL MOON

'Ar Hyd y Nos'/'All Through the Night'
Traditional, arr. Richard Barnard

A Welsh lullaby written by John Ceiriog Hughes in the late
19th century, and understandably popular with Welsh male
voice choirs, this is often sung for St David's Day, which falls
on 1st March. It has been variously translated into English
or given unrelated English words throughout its history, and
the English version given here is not a direct translation of
the Welsh original. It is based roughly on a version by Harold
Boulton but with some lines brought a little closer in meaning
to the Welsh version.

♩ = 84

Holl am - ran - tau'r sêr ddy-we-dant ar hyd y nos.
Stars and moon will sing a-bove thee all through the night.

Dy - ma'r ffordd i fro go-go-niant ar hyd y nos.
God will lend his an - gels to thee all through the night.

Go-lau a - rall yw ty-wy-llwch, I ar-ddan gos gwir bryd-fer-thwch,
Soft the drea-ming hours are cree-ping, hill and vale in dark - ness slee-ping,

Teu - lu'r ne-foedd mewn ta-we-lwch ar hyd y nos.
I will stay, my watch a-kee-ping all through the night.

April

1   April Fools' Day

5   Palm Sunday (Christian)

9   First day of Passover/Pesach (Jewish) – festivities begin the evening before

10   Good Friday (Christian) – bank holiday, England, Wales, Scotland, Northern Ireland

12   Easter Sunday (Christian)

13   Easter Monday (Christian) – bank holiday England, Wales, Northern Ireland and the Republic of Ireland

17   Orthodox Good Friday (Orthodox)

19   Orthodox Easter Sunday (Orthodox)

21   Isra and Mi'raj (Muslim)

21   Yom Hashoah – Holocaust Remembrance Day (Jewish)

22   Earth Day

23   St George's Day – patron saint of England

23   Start of British asparagus season

23   Shakespeare Day – William Shakespeare's birthday

24   First day of Ramadan (Muslim) – begins at the sighting of the new moon the night before

THE MOON

Names for April's full moon – Budding Moon, New Shoots Moon, Seed Moon, Paschal Moon

The medieval names of the full moon often reference agricultural markers, and none more so than April's: Budding Moon, New Shoots Moon and Seed Moon, which neatly tell you everything you need to know about the atmosphere and thrust of this month. April is still, of course, the time for seed sowing, just as it would have been in medieval times. Under April's full moon on the 8th, the countryside is no longer bare with dark twigs and stems. A soft fuzz of brightest green covers the black branches, and fluffs of blackthorn and damson blossom are appearing, bright pinpricks of white in the moonlight. The nights are shortening, lightening and losing their sharp chill, and the seeds that fell to the ground last autumn are finding warming earth and moisture and are starting to germinate. This moon is also the Paschal Moon, the first full moon after the spring equinox and the date by which Easter is calculated.

Moon phases

1st quarter – *1st April, 10.21*

Full moon – *8th April, 02.35*

3rd quarter – *14th April, 22.56*

New moon – *23rd April, 02.26*

1st quarter – *30th April, 20.38*

Moonrise and set

	Lowestoft		Dunquin		
	Rise	Set	Rise	Set	
1st	10.45	03.04	11.38	03.53	1st quarter
2nd	11.47	03.58	12.40	04.46	
3rd	13.01	04.41	13.54	05.29	
4th	14.23	05.16	15.16	06.04	
5th	15.49	05.43	16.42	06.32	
6th	17.18	06.07	18.10	06.56	
7th	18.47	06.28	19.39	07.17	
8th	20.16	06.48	21.08	07.38	full moon
9th	21.45	07.09	22.36	08.00	
10th	23.12	07.34	–	08.24	
11th	–	08.03	00.02	08.54	
12th	00.33	08.39	01.23	09.31	
13th	01.45	09.25	02.34	10.17	
14th	02.45	10.20	03.33	11.13	3rd quarter
15th	03.31	11.23	04.19	12.16	
16th	04.06	12.31	04.55	13.24	
17th	04.34	13.40	05.22	14.33	
18th	04.44	14.49	05.43	15.41	
19th	05.13	15.57	06.02	16.49	
20th	05.29	17.05	06.18	17.56	
21st	05.43	18.12	06.33	19.03	
22nd	05.58	19.20	06.48	20.10	
23rd	06.14	20.28	07.04	21.19	new moon
24th	06.31	21.38	07.22	22.28	
25th	06.53	22.48	07.43	23.38	
26th	07.19	23.57	08.11	–	
27th	07.54	–	08.46	00.46	
28th	08.39	01.00	09.31	01.49	
29th	09.36	01.56	10.29	02.44	
30th	10.44	02.41	11.37	03.30	1st quarter

Where moonset times are before moonrise times, this is the setting of the previous night's moon.

Gardening by the moon

New moon to 1st quarter: 1st and 23rd–30th. Sow crops that develop below ground. Dig the soil.

1st quarter to full moon: 1st–8th. Sow crops that develop above ground. Plant seedlings and young plants.

Full moon to 3rd quarter: 8th–14th. Harvest crops for immediate eating. Harvest fruit.

3rd quarter to new moon: 14th–23rd. Prune. Harvest for storage. Fertilise and mulch the soil.

April moon dates

8th – full moon: Buddhist New Year. This is also Abhidhamma Day, celebrating Buddha's descent from heaven, which he visited in order to teach his mother.

8th and 23rd – full moon and new moon: best fishing days. Some fishermen believe that fish bite best in the 45 minutes either side of moonrise and set on the full and new moons. So that would be 90 minutes from 06.03 and 19.31 on the 8th, and from 05.29 and 19.43 on the 23rd (Lowestoft times).

8th – the Paschal Moon. The first full moon after the spring equinox is the Paschal Moon, and Easter Sunday falls on the first Sunday after this.

23rd – new moon in Taurus. This month's new moon is in Taurus, an earthy and steady sign – astrologers believe this is a good moment for planning projects of a practical nature. These plans will come to fruition around the time that the full moon is in Taurus, on 31st October.

24th (predicted) – day after the sighting of the new crescent moon: the start of Ramadan. Ramadan is the holiest month in the Islamic year. It is the month in which the Quran was revealed to the prophet Muhammad, and Muslims fast from dawn to sunset throughout the month.

25th – day after the calculated first sighting of the new crescent moon: the start of Iyar. The name for this Hebrew month comes from *ayyaru*, meaning 'blossom'.

Supermoon

The moon's orbit around the earth is elliptical, that is to say
that it is not a perfect circle, and doesn't keep the moon a
set distance away from us all the way through each month.
During every month the moon has a moment of perigee,
when it is at its closest to us, and a moment of apogee, when
it is farthest away. When these perigees coincide with a full
moon, the moon looks larger and brighter than it normally
does and is called a supermoon, although the correct name
would be perigee full moon. The full moon on 8th April will
occur when it is at its closest point in its orbit this month,
at 357,030km away, and so should appear up to 14 per cent
larger and up to 30 per cent brighter than it does when it is
at its farthest away. The opposite – a mini moon, or apogee
full moon – will occur on 31st October, when the moon
will be 406,166km away, a difference of nearly 50,000km.

THE SKY

At night

1st Close approach of Mars and Saturn, visible from 05.00 at an altitude of 13 degrees above the southeastern horizon until lost in the dawn at 06.30.

8th Supermoon. At 357,030km away, this is the closest the moon will be to us while full this year (see page 81).

15th Close approach of the moon, Jupiter and Saturn, visible from 04.00 low in the southeastern sky until lost in the dawn at 06.00.

16th Close approach of the moon and Mars, visible from 05.00 low in the southeastern sky until lost in the dawn at 6.00.

21st Lyrids meteor shower. Dust from Comet Thatcher burning up as it hits our atmosphere causes this slow burn of a meteor shower. Not particularly spectacular but if you are lucky you may spot its occasional persistent ionised gas trails that glow for a few seconds. Peaks on the night of the 21st and early hours of the 22nd.

26th Close approach of Moon and Venus in the west at dusk at an altitude of 29 degrees. Visible from about 19.30 until setting at 22.30.

By day

The sun reaches an altitude of 50 degrees in the London sky and 46 degrees in the Glasgow sky at solar midday (13.00 BST/IST) on 21st April.

Day length increases by 1h 54m in Lowestoft, Suffolk, and by 1h 53m in Dunquin, Republic of Ireland.

Earliest sunrise: 30th April, Lowestoft 05.23, Dunquin 06.12.

Latest sunset: 30th April, Lowestoft 20.18, Dunquin 21.06.

Sunrise and set

	Lowestoft		Dunquin	
	Rise	Set	Rise	Set
1st	06.26	19.27	07.15	20.16
2nd	06.24	19.29	07.13	20.18
3rd	06.21	19.31	07.11	20.19
4th	06.19	19.33	07.08	20.21
5th	06.17	19.34	07.06	20.23
6th	06.14	19.36	07.04	20.25
7th	06.12	19.38	07.01	20.26
8th	06.10	19.40	06.59	20.28
9th	06.08	19.41	06.57	20.30
10th	06.05	19.43	06.55	20.31
11th	06.03	19.45	06.52	20.33
12th	06.01	19.47	06.50	20.35
13th	05.59	19.48	06.48	20.37
14th	05.56	19.50	06.46	20.38
15th	05.54	19.52	06.44	20.40
16th	05.52	19.54	06.41	20.42
17th	05.50	19.55	06.39	20.44
18th	05.48	19.57	06.37	20.45
19th	05.45	19.59	06.35	20.47
20th	05.43	20.01	06.33	20.49
21st	05.41	20.02	06.31	20.50
22nd	05.39	20.04	06.29	20.52
23rd	05.37	20.06	06.26	20.54
24th	05.35	20.08	06.24	20.56
25th	05.33	20.09	06.22	20.57
26th	05.31	20.11	06.20	20.59
27th	05.29	20.13	06.18	21.01
28th	05.27	20.14	06.16	21.02
29th	05.25	20.16	06.14	21.04
30th	05.23	20.18	06.12	21.06

A

THE SEA

Average sea temperature

Ayr:	8.6°C
Sunderland:	8.1°C
Dingle:	10.6°C
Dublin:	9.1°C
Aberystwyth:	9.4°C
Lowestoft:	8.6°C
Poole:	9.9°C
Newquay:	10.6°C

Spring and neap tides

The spring tides are the most extreme tides of the month, with the highest rises and falls, and the neap tides are the least extreme, with the smallest. Exact timings vary around the coast, but expect them around the following dates:

Spring tides: 10th–11th and 26th–27th

Neap tides: 2nd–3rd and 16th–17th

In the tide timetable opposite, spring tides are shown with an asterisk.

April tide timetable for Dover

For guidance on how to convert this for your local area, see page 8.

| | *High water* | | *Low water* | |
	Morning	Afternoon	Morning	Afternoon
1st	03.14	15.46	10.41	23.11
2nd	04.27	17.57	11.50	–
3rd	06.44	19.22	00.45	13.44
4th	07.55	20.24	02.20	15.00
5th	08.53	21.16	03.29	16.04
6th	09.42	22.03	04.31	17.03
7th	10.27	22.47	05.31	17.58
8th	11.09	23.29	06.25	18.47
9th	11.50	–	07.13	19.30
10th*	00.10	12.31	07.55	20.08
11th*	00.53	13.13	08.33	20.45
12th	01.36	13.57	09.10	21.23
13th	02.21	14.46	09.47	22.03
14th	03.12	15.41	10.30	22.53
15th	04.12	16.45	11.27	–
16th	05.23	18.02	00.02	12.43
17th	07.14	19.36	01.25	14.02
18th	08.39	20.44	02.47	15.18
19th	09.26	21.30	03.58	16.19
20th	10.02	22.08	04.50	17.05
21st	10.33	22.41	05.30	17.42
22nd	11.00	23.12	06.02	18.11
23rd	11.28	23.39	06.29	18.38
24th	11.54	–	06.56	19.06
25th	00.02	12.17	07.24	19.36
26th*	00.25	12.40	07.54	20.07
27th*	00.51	13.09	08.24	20.39
28th	01.24	13.46	08.56	21.15
29th	02.06	14.34	09.34	21.58
30th	02.58	15.37	10.23	22.56

A

TYPES OF STARFISH

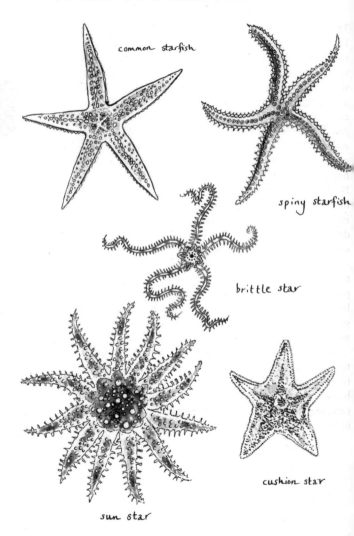

common starfish

spiny starfish

brittle star

sun star

cushion star

NATURE

The hedgerow in April

Last month a few buds appeared over the dark brown twigginess of the hedgerow, but during the showery and ever-warming month of April the hazel, blackthorn and hawthorn start to properly green up, joined by a general unfurling and uncurling of soft shield fern, western polypody, male fern and hart's-tongue fern, all along the damp hedge bottom. And here comes the blossom in abundance: wild cherry, elder and the start of the great hawthorn blooming, now visited by green-veined white, holly blue, orange tip and speckled wood butterflies, all starting to emerge from winter chrysalises. Northern hedgerows will see sweet cicely, too. Red-tailed bumblebee queens are visiting all of the flowers – which now include jack-by-the-hedge, starry white greater stitchwort and dog violet, and the first of the bluebells – to fuel up after they emerge from their winter hibernation underground.

By night, badger cubs start to explore around the entrance to their sett, staying close to their mother. Bank voles are producing their first litters of the season from their grass-lined nests beneath the roots. Stoats produce one litter per year around now, kept cosy during the unpredictable spring weather in their fur-lined burrows.

Pairs of chaffinches have started building their nests together, lining them with softest moss, wool and feathers so that the female can lay three to six pale eggs splotched with brownish red. Greenfinches are taking much less fastidious care, making a rough-and-ready nest in dense, bushy parts of the hedgerow in which to raise their own broods this year.

THE FLOWER GARDEN

April's flower garden picking prompts

A little glass of blues – forget-me-nots, pulmonaria and grape
hyacinths; a posy of fritillaries and anemones; blossom and
pussy willow in a big vase.

Jobs in the flower garden

- Peonies are the most luxurious cut flowers that you can
  grow yourself. Their season is brief but glorious, and if
  you can squeeze a plant in, do. You will be so glad, for
  a few weeks a year. Buy bare root plants now and plant
  them out immediately. 'Coral Charm' is a soft salmon
  pink and fully double, 'Immaculée' is pure white with
  two distinct rings of petals, while 'Sarah Bernhardt' is
  softest pink.
- In a greenhouse or on an inside windowsill, sow half-
  hardy annuals for picking: snapdragon, zinnia, nicotiana,
  cleome, cosmos and tithonia. Sow them into modules
  for easy potting on or planting out. Plant out sweet
  peas alongside shrubby 'peasticks' or nets for them to
  scramble up.
- Pot up dahlia tubers and protect them from frosts. They
  will need to be grown in a cold frame or greenhouse until
  ready to plant out after frosts have passed, in another
  month or so. Once they are planted, protect them from
  slugs while they are young.

THE KITCHEN GARDEN

The big job for April is second early and maincrop potato planting, as they need to be in the ground by the end of the month. This is your last chance to sow tomatoes and aubergines, though you can still buy and plant small ones later. Make this month's sowings of beetroot and salad leaves under cloches, but the soil should now be just about warm enough for other sowings to be made without cover. Use your judgement on this, and in very cold weather wait a while. You can also start planting out your hardier seedlings this month. Again use your judgement and only plant them out if the weather is fairly mild. These seedlings will need to be 'hardened off' before planting out: gradually acclimatise them to the outdoors by placing them outdoors for increasingly long spells. Protect against slugs as you do, as they can be devastating this month.

Sowing and planting crops

Fruit/veg	Sow under cover	Sow direct	Plant
Aubergines	✓*		
Tomatoes	✓*		
Sweet peppers	✓*		
Melons	✓*		
Courgettes	✓		
Summer squash	✓		
Pumpkins	✓		
Winter squash	✓		
Cucumbers	✓		
Sweetcorn	✓		
Florence fennel	✓		✓
French beans	✓	✓	✓
Runner beans	✓		
Gherkins	✓		✓
Summer cabbages	✓		✓
Autumn cabbages	✓		✓
Winter cabbages	✓		

Fruit/veg	Sow under cover	Sow direct	Plant
Kohlrabi		✓	✓
Sprouting broccoli		✓	✓
Calabrese		✓	
Kale	✓		✓
Summer cauliflowers	✓		✓
Autumn cauliflowers	✓		✓
Brussels sprouts		✓	✓
Celeriac	✓		
Celery	✓		
Lettuces	✓	✓	✓
Salad leaves	✓	✓	
Spring onions		✓	
Chicory and radicchio	✓		
Spinach and Swiss chard		✓	✓
Beetroot		✓	✓
Coriander		✓	
Chives		✓	
Dill		✓	
Parsley		✓	
Fennel (leaf)		✓	
Carrots		✓	
Turnips		✓	
Radishes		✓	
Broad beans		✓	✓
Runner beans	✓	✓	
French beans	✓	✓	
Peas		✓	✓
Second early and maincrop potatoes			✓
Onion and shallot sets			✓
Garlic			✓
Asparagus			✓
Globe and Jerusalem artichokes			✓

*In heated propagator

THE KITCHEN

Sauce of the month – *skordalia*

This sauce is traditionally eaten in Greece during Lent, with slices of fried aubergine and courgette or with vegetable fritters making an entirely meatless meal. Boil two large potatoes until tender and, while still hot, either pass them through a ricer or mash them. Put three cloves of crushed garlic into a food processor along with 65g roughly chopped blanched almonds, 50ml water and the juice of half a lemon. Measure out 240ml extra virgin olive oil and pour in enough to just cover the almonds. Blitz until smooth, then add the rest of the oil and blitz again. Stir into the potato, season with plenty of salt and pepper, and serve.

In season

Vegetables: Jersey royal potatoes, nettles, radishes, first early spears of asparagus, rocket, sorrel, spring onions, purple sprouting broccoli, winter lettuces, spring cabbages, salad leaves, spinach, leeks, spring cauliflowers, Swiss chard
Herbs: parsley, chervil, coriander
Fruit: rhubarb
Meat: spring lamb
Fish: halibut, crab, salmon, shrimp, whitebait, lobster

A

RECIPES

Little Lagos' baked cumin frejon beans for Good Friday
By Yemisi Aribisala

South London is sometimes called Little Lagos, as it is the nucleus of the Nigerian community in the UK, and there are hundreds of black majority churches in the area. Housed in old bingo halls and warehouses, they are all bursting at the seams on a Sunday, vibrant and happy with Pentecostal effervescence.

Among them are the Yoruba Catholics. Holy Week is an important time for the community, and Good Friday has a sober, reflective quality – most people fast and so can only partake of meatless meals. Frejon beans is a soup traditionally eaten on the day, perhaps with fried plantains, charred sweet pepper stew, baked mackerel fillets and cooked attieke.

Serves 4, generously
Ingredients
A generous tablespoon of whole cloves
1.7 litres water
350g black eye beans
250g turtle beans
4 tablespoons apple cider vinegar
2 teaspoons cumin seeds
1 large onion, finely chopped
1 scotch bonnet, finely chopped
2 cloves garlic, crushed or finely chopped
2 teaspoons edible shea butter
50g creamed coconut
50g coconut sugar
130ml coconut milk
raw cacao powder (optional)

A

Method

The night before, make clove tea. Put the cloves in a pan with the measured water and bring to the boil. Remove from the heat and leave to brew overnight. Put the black eye beans and turtle beans in a big pan of water with 1 tablespoon of apple cider vinegar, and soak overnight.

The next day, drain and rinse the beans. Put them in a pan and cover with water, bring to the boil and simmer briskly for 45 minutes. Preheat your oven to 200°C, Gas Mark 6. Put the cumin seeds in a deep ovenproof dish, and place in the oven while it heats up. Once the seeds turn dark and the smell is earthy and sweet, take the dish out of the oven. Crush the seeds between your fingers to release their sweet dense aroma, and return to the dish. Once the beans are cooked, drain them and place them on top of the cumin seeds.

In a large frying pan, sauté the onion, scotch bonnet and garlic gently in the shea butter until you have a soft, bubbly, velvety mass (do not brown the ingredients at all). Tip the contents of the pan onto the beans. Pour 2 pints of clove tea over the beans, along with the creamed coconut, the remaining apple cider vinegar and the coconut sugar. Stir well.

Cover the dish and place in the oven. Cook for 3½–4 hours, until the beans are softened, checking regularly to make sure the dish doesn't become dry. Add more clove tea if needed.

Remove the dish from the oven and leave to cool. Blend the beans with the remaining clove tea until very smooth – you should have about 150ml clove tea to 250g cooked beans. In batches, pass the blended beans through a sieve and then put into a large pan.

On a very low heat, warm the soup through with the coconut milk. Once warm, pour into bowls, sprinkle with raw cacao powder (optional) and serve.

RECIPES

Easter *pasha*

This recipe comes from Angela Morris and Tim Homewood of Homewood Cheeses in Somerset. It is an Easter dish originally from the Russian Orthodox community, and traditionally eaten with a spiced bread known as *kulich*, which was shaped to represent a priest's hat, as was the *pasha* itself. Tim and Angela make it once a year from their ewe's curd cheese for the Saturday market before Easter, and they recommend that it is eaten spread on toasted hot cross buns. You can track down their ewe's curd via Daylesford nationwide, or make your own curds using the method for Yorkshire Curd Tart for Whitsun (see page 115).

Serves 6

Ingredients

50g softened unsalted butter

50g caster sugar

100g curds

30g ground almonds

90g raisins

50g candied peel, finely chopped

2 tablespoons soured cream

Method

Cream the butter and the sugar together until fluffy, then add the rest of the ingredients and mix well. Line a tall mould (a new flowerpot would be perfect) with muslin, and spoon the mixture in, pushing it down with the back of the spoon. Fold the corners in and place a weight on top, then refrigerate for 12 hours before turning out and serving.

CHARM OF THE MONTH

Coloured eggs for Easter

Easter's association with eggs is one of the great threads that stretches from the present back into the ancient past. We know that eggs are partly associated with Easter because egg-free Lent created a backlog to be eaten, decorated and rolled down hills with joyful abandon on Easter Sunday. However, there may be far older, pagan associations connected to the feeling of rebirth and fertility that comes with the equinox and with moving out of the dark half of the year and into the light. Decorating eggs has a long and certainly pre-Christian tradition in Eastern Europe and Persia. The earliest record of it in the British Isles is in the 13th century, when King Edward I ordered 450 eggs to be decorated as Easter gifts, though the practice may well have been going on unrecorded for some time before that.

To decorate an egg, first make a small hole at the top and another at the bottom. Put your mouth to the top hole and blow the egg contents into a bowl (saving them for an eggy dish). Wash the egg through and then paint, felt-tip or stick designs on it. Give decorated eggs to friends and family as a symbol of this hopeful and expectant moment in the year.

A

A SONG FOR APRIL'S FULL MOON

'The Rising of the Moon'
By John Keegan Casey, arr. Richard Barnard

The role of the moon in this evocative Irish ballad was to act as a secret signal, something all those in the know could look out for, to rise in unified rebellion: 'the pikes must be together at the rising of the moon'. It was written by John Keegan Casey in 1866 about the doomed 1798 Rebellion, a battle between the United Irishmen and the British Army.

♩ = 92

Oh, come tell me, Sean O' - Fa- rrell, tell me why you hu-rry so? "Hush, m

bhua -chaill, hush and lis- ten," and his eyes were all a - glow "I bea

or - ders from the cap- tain, get you rea - dy quick and soon with you

pike u - pon your shoul- der at the ri - sing of the moon. At the

ri - sing of the moon,_ at the ri - sing of the moon, with you

pike u - pon your shoul- der at the ri - sing of the moon."

Oh, come tell me, Sean O'Farrell, tell me why you hurry so?
'Hush, my bhuachaill, hush and listen,' and his eyes were all aglow
'I bear orders from the captain, get you ready quick and soon
With your pike upon your shoulder at the rising of the moon.
At the rising of the moon, at the rising of the moon
With your pike upon your shoulder at the rising of the moon.'

Tell me, tell me, Sean O'Farrell, where the gathering is to be?
'Near the old spot by the river, right well known to you and me.'
One last word, the signal token? 'Whistle out the marching tune
For our pikes must be together by the rising of the moon.
By the rising of the moon, by the rising of the moon
For our pikes must be together by the rising of the moon.'

Out from many mud-walled cabins, eyes were looking through
    the night
Many manly hearts were beating for the blessed morning light.
A cry was heard along the river, like some banshee's mournful
    croon
And a thousand pikes were flashing by the rising of the moon.
By the rising of the moon, by the rising of the moon
And a thousand pikes were flashing by the rising of the moon.

All along the shining river one dark mass of men was seen
And above them in the night sky flew their own immortal green.
Death to every foe and traitor! Onward, strike the marching tune
And hurrah my boys for freedom, 'tis the rising of the moon.
'Tis the rising of the moon, 'tis the rising of the moon
And hurrah my boys for freedom, 'tis the rising of the moon.

May

- **1** May Day/Beltane (pagan/neopagan)
- **1** International Workers' Day
- **4** Early May bank holiday, Scotland and Republic of Ireland
- **8** Victory in Europe (VE) Day, 75th anniversary – bank holiday in England, Wales and Northern Ireland
- **9** Liberation Day, observance, Jersey and Guernsey
- **17** Rogation Sunday, beating the bounds (Christian, traditional)
- **19** Laylat al Qadr – the Night of Power (Muslim)
- **21** Ascension Day, Holy Thursday
- **21** Stow Horse Fair – spring gypsy/Roma/traveller gathering
- **24** Eid al-Fitr – celebration of the end of Ramadan (Muslim)
- **25** Spring bank holiday – England, Wales, Scotland and Northern Ireland
- **29** Feast of Weeks/Shavuot (Jewish) – festivities begin at sundown on 28th
- **31** Whit Sunday/Whitsun/Pentecost (Christian)

THE MOON

Names for May's full moon – Mother's Moon, Bright Moon

In May the light of the full moon is reflected back by reams of hawthorn hedges all blossoming white at once. Hawthorn was for hundreds of years the farmers' hedge of choice, and was used to create stock-proof (and people-proof) enclosures, and so the English countryside in particular is alight with sprays of pure white blossom this month. Some Algonquian tribes of North America call May's moon the Flower Moon, and this is certainly a time of floral abundance in the countryside and gardens. The bees and butterflies will be out pollinating the flowers and making the most of the abundant nectar in the daytime, just as the moths will at night. As night comes to an end and dawn breaks, this is the time when the songbirds are at their most vocal, marking out their territories and impressing mates. The hedgerow is a cacophony as the full moon sets and the sun rises. It is a fertile time and a time for making babies – the medieval name for May's full moon was Mother's Moon, which may refer to the goddess Maia after whom May is named and who was associated with midwives, motherhood and nursing.

Moon phases

Full moon – *7th May, 10.45*

3rd quarter – *14th May, 14.03*

New moon – *22nd May, 17.39*

1st quarter – *30th May, 03.30*

Moonrise and set

	Lowestoft		*Dunquin*		
	Rise	Set	Rise	Set	
1st	12.01	03.18	12.54	04.06	
2nd	13.23	03.46	14.16	04.35	
3rd	14.48	04.10	15.40	04.59	
4th	16.14	04.31	17.06	05.20	
5th	17.42	04.50	18.33	05.40	
6th	19.10	05.10	20.01	06.00	
7th	20.39	05.32	21.30	06.22	full moon
8th	22.05	05.58	22.55	06.49	
9th	23.25	06.31	–	07.22	
10th	–	07.12	00.14	08.05	
11th	00.33	08.05	01.22	08.58	
12th	01.27	09.07	02.15	10.00	
13th	02.08	10.15	02.56	11.08	
14th	02.38	11.26	03.26	12.19	3rd quarter
15th	03.02	12.36	03.50	13.29	
16th	03.20	13.45	04.09	14.37	
17th	03.37	14.53	04.26	15.45	
18th	03.51	16.01	04.41	16.52	
19th	04.06	17.08	04.55	17.59	
20th	04.21	18.17	05.11	19.07	
21st	04.38	19.27	05.28	20.17	
22nd	04.57	20.38	05.48	21.28	new moon
23rd	05.22	21.48	06.13	22.37	
24th	05.54	22.54	06.46	23.43	
25th	06.35	23.53	07.28	–	
26th	07.29	–	08.22	00.42	
27th	08.34	00.42	09.27	01.31	
28th	09.48	01.21	10.41	02.09	
29th	11.08	01.52	12.00	02.40	
30th	12.30	02.16	13.22	03.05	1st quarter
31st	13.54	02.37	14.45	03.26	

Where moonset times are before moonrise times, this is the setting of the previous night's moon.

Gardening by the moon

1st quarter to full moon: 1st–7th and 30th–31st. Sow crops that develop above ground. Plant seedlings and young plants.

Full moon to 3rd quarter: 7th–14th. Harvest crops for immediate eating. Harvest fruit.

3rd quarter to new moon: 14th–22nd. Prune. Harvest for storage. Fertilise and mulch the soil.

New moon to 1st quarter: 22nd–30th. Sow crops that develop below ground. Dig the soil.

May moon dates

7th – full moon: Vesak, Buddha Day. A day when Buddhists celebrate Buddha's birth, life and death. It is a day for special efforts to bring happiness to the aged and the sick, by visiting and giving gifts.

7th and 22nd – full moon and new moon: best fishing days. Some fishermen believe that fish bite best in the 45 minutes either side of moonrise and set on the full and new moons. So that would be 90 minutes from 04.47 and 19.54 on the 7th, and from 04.12 and 19.53 on the 22nd (Lowestoft times).

22nd – new moon in Gemini. This month's new moon is in Gemini, the sign governing communication – astrologers believe this is a good moment for beginning projects that involve dialogue, broadcasting and generally making connections. These plans will reach fruition around the time the full moon is next in Gemini, on 30th November.

24th – day after the calculated first sighting of the new crescent moon: the start of Sivan. This is the start of the Hebrew month Sivan, which means 'season' or 'time'.

24th (predicted) – day after the sighting of the new crescent moon: the start of Shawwal. The first day of the Islamic month of Shawwal is Eid al-Fitr, a day of feasting and celebration to mark the end of Ramadan.

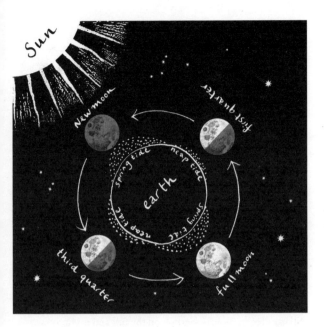

The moon and the tides

It is the gravitational force of the moon in the sky above us
that pulls the water of the earth up towards it and causes our
daily tides (though see page 169 for why there are two tides a
day, rather than one). But we are also affected by the sun. It is
when the sun and the moon team up that we can most notice
its effect, and this happens at new moon and full moon, when
sun, moon and earth are all in a straight line. The cooperation
creates particularly extreme tides twice a month, reaching
high up the shore and then falling back to their lowest point,
revealing seabed that is usually covered; these tides are called
spring tides. When the moon is at first and third quarter, it is
at right angles with the sun. Each cancels the other out, and
the tides – called neap tides – have their smallest rises and falls
of the month.

THE SKY

At night

5th Eta Aquarids meteor shower. Up to 30 meteors per hour (though more often around ten per hour) as we pass through the dust trail of Halley's Comet. Peaks late night on the 5th and early morning of the 6th. The moon being almost full will make for tricky spotting conditions.

12th Close approach of the moon, Jupiter and Saturn, visible from 02.00 low in the southern sky until lost in the dawn at 05.00.

15th Close approach of the moon and Mars, visible low in southeastern sky from 03.30 until lost in the dawn at 05.00.

24th Close approach of the moon and Venus, visible low in the northwestern sky from about 21.00 until 22.00.

By day

The sun reaches an altitude of 59 degrees in the London sky and 55 degrees in the Glasgow sky at solar midday (13.00 BST/IST) on 21st.

Day length increases by 1h 29m in Lowestoft, Suffolk, and by 1h 28m in Dunquin, Republic of Ireland.

Earliest sunrise: 31st May, Lowestoft 04.37, Dunquin 05.27.

Latest sunset: 31st May, Lowestoft 21.05, Dunquin 21.52.

Sunrise and set

	Lowestoft		*Dunquin*	
	Rise	Set	Rise	Set
1st	05.21	20.20	06.11	21.07
2nd	05.19	20.21	06.09	21.09
3rd	05.17	20.23	06.07	21.11
4th	05.15	20.25	06.05	21.12
5th	05.13	20.26	06.03	21.14
6th	05.11	20.28	06.01	21.16
7th	05.09	20.30	05.59	21.17
8th	05.08	20.31	05.58	21.19
9th	05.06	20.33	05.56	21.21
10th	05.04	20.35	05.54	21.22
11th	05.03	20.36	05.53	21.24
12th	05.01	20.38	05.51	21.25
13th	04.59	20.40	05.49	21.27
14th	04.58	20.41	05.48	21.29
15th	04.56	20.43	05.46	21.30
16th	04.55	20.44	05.45	21.32
17th	04.53	20.46	05.43	21.33
18th	04.52	20.47	05.42	21.35
19th	04.50	20.49	05.41	21.36
20th	04.49	20.50	05.39	21.37
21st	04.48	20.52	05.38	21.39
22nd	04.46	20.53	05.37	21.40
23rd	04.45	20.55	05.35	21.42
24th	04.44	20.56	05.34	21.43
25th	04.43	20.57	05.33	21.44
26th	04.41	20.59	05.32	21.46
27th	04.40	21.00	05.31	21.47
28th	04.39	21.01	05.30	21.48
29th	04.38	21.02	05.29	21.49
30th	04.37	21.04	05.28	21.51
31st	04.37	21.05	05.27	21.52

M

THE SEA

Average sea temperature

Ayr:	9.9°C
Sunderland:	9.7°C
Dingle:	11.7°C
Dublin:	10.4°C
Aberystwyth:	10.9°C
Lowestoft:	11.0°C
Poole:	11.4°C
Newquay:	11.9°C

Spring and neap tides

The spring tides are the most extreme tides of the month, with the highest rises and falls, and the neap tides are the least extreme, with the smallest. Exact timings vary around the coast, but expect them around the following dates:

Spring tides: 9th–10th and 25th–26th

Neap tides: 1st–2nd and 15th–16th

In the tide timetable opposite, spring tides are shown with an asterisk.

May tide timetable for Dover

For guidance on how to convert this for your local area, see page 8.

| | *High water* | | *Low water* | |
	Morning	Afternoon	Morning	Afternoon
1st	04.20	17.27	11.30	–
2nd	06.20	18.52	00.23	13.14
3rd	07.32	19.56	01.53	14.31
4th	08.30	20.51	03.00	15.34
5th	09.20	21.39	04.03	16.34
6th	10.06	22.25	05.04	17.30
7th	10.49	23.09	06.01	18.21
8th	11.31	23.51	06.50	19.06
9th*	–	12.12	07.33	19.47
10th*	00.34	12.55	08.13	20.27
11th	01.18	13.40	08.51	21.06
12th	02.04	14.28	09.29	21.48
13th	02.54	15.20	10.10	22.36
14th	03.51	16.18	11.02	23.38
15th	04.54	17.23	–	12.11
16th	06.12	18.39	00.51	13.23
17th	07.43	19.53	02.01	14.28
18th	08.39	20.46	03.03	15.25
19th	09.19	21.28	03.55	16.14
20th	09.53	22.03	04.38	16.55
21st	10.24	22.35	05.16	17.31
22nd	10.54	23.05	05.51	18.06
23rd	11.24	23.33	06.26	18.41
24th	11.52	–	07.01	19.16
25th*	00.03	12.23	07.35	19.51
26th*	00.36	12.59	08.09	20.28
27th	01.14	13.41	08.45	21.07
28th	02.00	14.33	09.26	21.53
29th	02.58	15.38	10.15	22.51
30th	04.16	16.56	11.20	–

SONGBIRDS

chiffchaff

blackbird

mistle thrush

wren

blue tit

NATURE

The hedgerow in May

This month the vibrant lime green of the hedgerow is all but eclipsed by white froth. Hawthorn – the plant that dominates our hedgerows – is in explosive, pure white flower, but then so is cow parsley, wayfaring tree and elder. It's a symphony of white. There is vibrant colour to be found, too, though. Bluebells are at their peak, and they are joined by pink herb Robert, acid-green Alexanders, purple dog violets and fat golden dandelions all along the hedgerow bottom. Large cabbage white, orange tip and holly blue butterflies visit them for nectar, while the overwintering population of red admiral butterflies is bolstered this month by a great influx of migrants fluttering over from mainland Europe. They mate and lay their eggs on the tips of the nettle leaves. Magpie moths are emerging, taking to the wing, and laying eggs, and their larvae feast on young hawthorn leaves.

Badger cubs come out and explore, sometimes even in the daytime. May is the beginning of the main hedgehog rutting season, though some will have started in April. Pygmy shrews – which live in tunnels beneath the hedgerow and feed on beetles, caterpillars, worms and woodlice – are mating now and will produce the first of up to four litters in a month's time. Dormice finally emerge from hibernation this month, though they will go back into a state of dormancy at the drop of a hat if there are food shortages or bad weather. They weave bark and leaves into a summer nest high up in the hedgerow, emerging at night to forage for spring flowers.

THE FLOWER GARDEN

May's flower garden picking prompts

Cow parsley from the hedgerow and tulips from the garden;
a few stems of lilac in a vase; a little bunch of lily of the
valley in a glass.

Jobs in the flower garden

- It is time to plant up hanging baskets, pots and window
  boxes for gloriously colourful displays of summer
  bedding. Find ranks of little plants in every garden centre,
  and choose from Surfinia petunias, lobelias, pelargoniums,
  begonias and fuchsias, mixing them in with foliage plants
  to trail, soften and flatter. They will grow a lot, and fast,
  so don't pack them in too tightly.
- Plant out your hardy and half-hardy annuals, sown
  indoors earlier this year – cornflowers, marigolds,
  nasturtiums, sunflowers and all. Space them out and
  protect them from slugs. If you sowed directly into the
  soil, you will need to thin out the resulting seedlings now.
- Gladioli bulbs can go into pots or the ground now to flower
  later in the summer. *Gladiolus communis* subsp. *byzantinus*
  is a delicately shaped flower in a vivid purple, *G.* × *colvillei*
  'The Bride' is a similar shape in pure white. You can stagger
  their flowering times by planting handfuls of the bulbs
  every week or so over the next couple of months.

CHARM OF THE MONTH

Primroses for the fairies

Belief in fairies was strong throughout the British Isles well
into the 19th century, from the *aos sìth* of Scotland and the
aos sí of Ireland to the *tylwyth teg* of Wales. We now think
of fairies as winged, delicate, harmless little creatures, but
the fairies of old were very much earthbound, and their dark
side was strong. While they could bring luck and blessings,
they were also fickle and easily angered, as well as being not
at all averse to a bit of child kidnapping or – possibly worse –
swapping in 'changelings' for healthy children. Sources claim
either the first three days of May or May Day Eve as the time
when fairies' wicked tendencies were to the fore. (Despite the
title, Shakespeare's *A Midsummer Night's Dream* – which
has put about the idea that midsummer is when the fairies
and humans intermingle – is actually set on May Day Eve.).
They could be expected to make a foray to at least steal some
butter, if not your actual first-born. In *A Treasury of British
Folklore*, Dee Dee Chainey writes that primroses have a
particular power against fairies, and no fairies can pass them,
so they should be scattered along the threshold during the first
few days of this month.

THE KITCHEN GARDEN

This is the month to start practising in earnest 'successional sowing', which means sowing little and often. Sow short rows of carrots, beetroot, radishes, spring onions, Florence fennel, kohlrabi, lettuces and other salad leaves every few weeks for a continuous supply. There will be lots of planting out this month. Make sure you take care to harden off plants first, by giving them progressively longer spells outside to get used to the difference. Tomatoes, chillies, courgettes, pumpkins, melons and cucumbers are tender and will need to be planted under cloches at first. Potatoes should all be in the ground or in pots by now, and you should earth them up as they grow.

Sowing and planting crops

Fruit/veg	Sow under cover	Sow direct	Plant
Aubergines			✓
Chillies			✓
Sweet peppers			✓
Tomatoes			✓
Courgettes	✓		✓
Summer squash	✓		✓
Pumpkins	✓		✓
Winter squash	✓		✓
Cucumbers		✓	✓
Melons	✓		✓
Gherkins	✓		✓
Sweetcorn		✓	✓
Florence fennel		✓	✓
French beans		✓	✓
Runner beans		✓	✓
Summer cabbages	✓		✓
Autumn cabbages	✓		✓
Winter cabbages	✓		
Kohlrabi	✓		✓

Fruit/veg	Sow under cover	Sow direct	Plant
Sprouting broccoli	✓		✓
Calabrese		✓	
Kale	✓		✓
Summer cauliflowers	✓		
Autumn cauliflowers	✓		
Brussels sprouts		✓	✓
Celeriac	✓		✓
Celery	✓		✓
Leeks		✓	✓
Lettuces	✓	✓	✓
Salad leaves	✓	✓	✓
Chicory and radicchio	✓		
Spring onions		✓	
Beetroot		✓	
Spinach and Swiss chard		✓	
Dill		✓	✓
Basil	✓	✓	✓
Fennel (leaf)		✓	✓
Carrots		✓	✓
Turnips		✓	✓
Radishes		✓	✓
Runner beans		✓	✓
French beans		✓	✓
Peas		✓	✓
Asparagus			✓
Globe artichokes			✓
Rhubarb			✓
Strawberries			✓

THE KITCHEN

Sauce of the month – *sauce gribiche* for asparagus
This sauce has elements in common with mayonnaise and with salad cream, but is far more interesting (and chunky) than either, and makes a lush accompaniment to steamed asparagus. You might also eat it with boiled Jersey potatoes, charred leeks, cold meats or any salad you like. Peel six hard-boiled eggs and put the yolks of two into a bowl (you won't need their whites, so keep these in the refrigerator to use in another dish) and mash them with the back of a fork. One at a time, mash the other whole eggs in, breaking up the whites as much as possible. Add half a tablespoon of white wine vinegar and mix it in, then start gradually adding 240ml extra virgin olive oil, tablespoon by tablespoon, mixing thoroughly to combine everything to a creamy consistency after each. Mix in a handful of chopped tarragon and a couple of tablespoons each of chopped capers and mini gherkins. Season with salt and pepper to taste. Serve immediately or chill and keep for up to a few days.

In season
Vegetables: Jersey royal potatoes, new potatoes from Ayrshire and Cornwall, broad beans, baby globe artichokes, green garlic, peas, young spinach, radishes, asparagus, sorrel, spring cabbages, spring cauliflowers, lettuces, turnips, Oriental leaves, spring onions
Herbs: chives and chive flowers, parsley, chervil
Fruit: rhubarb, the start of the strawberries
Meat: spring lamb
Fish: crab, sardine, plaice, mackerel

RECIPES

Yorkshire curd tart for Whitsun

Whitsun is the seventh Sunday after Easter, and it falls on 31st May this year. The week that follows it, Whitsuntide, was once a major holiday, marking a pause in the agricultural year as workers were given time off. The current spring bank holiday, which this year falls on 25th May, is a hangover from this. Whitsun and Whitsuntide were a time for fetes, fairs and Morris dancing, and are particularly associated with walks and races, and in Yorkshire with curd tarts. You can use curd cheese or ricotta instead of making your own curds, but the flavour is slightly sharper, and the curd-making is a very simple and satisfying thing to do if you have just a little time ahead of making the tarts.

Serves 8

Ingredients

For the curds (if making them yourself)

2 litres whole milk

50ml lemon juice

For the pastry

200g plain flour, plus extra for dusting

Pinch of salt

150g fridge-cold butter

2 teaspoons caster sugar

2 eggs

About 2 tablespoons cold water

For the filling

125g butter

60g golden caster sugar

250g store-bought curd cheese or ricotta (if not making
your own curds)

2 large eggs, beaten

Zest of 1 lemon

100g raisins

¼ teaspoon ground allspice or ¼ of a nutmeg, freshly
grated

1 teaspoon rosewater

Method
If you are making your own curds, start the night before. Heat
the milk in a pan until you see the first signs that it is about to
rise up the sides of the pan and come to the boil. Remove from
the heat and immediately stir in the lemon juice. It should start
to curdle straight away, but leave it for at least an hour to cool.
Pour into a sieve lined with a large piece of muslin. Gather
up the corners of the muslin and tie somewhere high with
a container below (such as around a high kitchen cupboard
handle, with a bowl below on the work surface). Leave to drip
and drain overnight. The next day, weigh out 250g of the curds
to use in the filling, and set aside.

To prepare the pastry, place the flour and salt in a large
bowl and grate in the butter. Rub in with your fingertips until
the mixture resembles fine breadcrumbs. Mix in the sugar and
1 egg. Add enough of the cold water to make a firm dough,
bringing it together with your hands. Knead briefly, then wrap
in clingfilm and refrigerate for 30 minutes. On a floured surface,
roll out the dough to about 2mm thick. Drape it over a rolling
pin and carefully place it in a 23cm loose-bottomed, fluted tart

tin. Gently push it into the corners using your fingertips or a small ball of leftover dough. Cut off the excess, leaving a little overhanging the top edge all around. Cover with clingfilm or a tea towel and refrigerate for at least 30 minutes.

Preheat the oven to 200°C, Gas Mark 6. Find a baking tray that is wider than the 23cm tart tin (or, if you don't have a large-enough tray, use a smaller tray upside down) and place it in the centre of the oven to heat up. Prick the base of the tart case with a fork. Cover with a sheet of baking parchment or kitchen foil, and then pour in rice or ceramic baking beans to hold the base down. Slide it onto the hot tray, and blind bake for 20 minutes. Remove from the oven and take off the parchment and rice or baking beans, and bake for a further 5 minutes.

Remove from the oven again, beat the remaining egg and paint the base and the sides of the pastry case with it, using a pastry brush. Return the pastry case to the oven for 5 minutes more, or until the base looks cooked through (at this point it can be a good idea to cover the edges with foil to stop them burning). Remove from the oven and, as soon as it is cool enough to handle, use a serrated knife held horizontally to gently saw off the excess pastry.

To make the filling, cream the butter and the sugar together until light and fluffy, then add the homemade curds or store-bought curd cheese or ricotta, along with the rest of the filling ingredients; mix well. Pour into the pastry case and return to the oven for 25–30 minutes, or until the top is set and golden. Cool on a wire rack for at least 15 minutes before serving.

A SONG FOR MAY'S FULL MOON

'Drink Down the Moon'
Traditional, arr. Richard Barnard

There are several alternative titles for this folk song, including 'The Bird in the Bush' and 'Three Maids a-Milking Did Go', and all are euphemistic in the extreme. The three maids very straightforwardly invite their male friend into the woods with them, without worrying about what anyone else might think ('Let the people say little or say much'). Here the moon, and particularly the idea of 'drinking down the moon', is a shorthand for surrendering to sensuality and passion.

Three maidens a-milking did go
Three maidens a-milking did go,
Oh, the wind it did blow high and the wind it did blow low
And it tossed their petticoats to and fro.

They met with a young man they did know
They met with a young man they did know
And they boldly asked of him if he had any skill
To catch them a small bird or two.

'Oh yes, I've a very fine skill
Oh yes, I've a very fine skill,
Won't you come along with me to the yonder flowering tree
And I'll catch you a small bird or two.'

So off to the green woods went they
So off to the green woods went they
And he tapped at the bush and the bird it did fly in
A little above her lily-white knee.

And her sparkling eyes they did turn round
Just as if she was all in a swound
And she cried 'I have a bird, and a very pretty bird
and he's pecking away at his own ground.'

Here's a health to the bird in the bush
Here's a health to the bird in the bush
And we'll drink up the sun, and we'll drink down the moon,
Let the people say little or say much.

M

June

- **1** Start of meteorological summer
- **1** Start of Pride Month
- **1** Start of Gypsy, Roma and Traveller History Month
- **1** June bank holiday, Republic of Ireland
- **4** 4th–10th: Appleby Horse Fair, Cumbria – gypsy/Roma/traveller gathering
- **7** Trinity Sunday (Christian)
- **11** Corpus Christi (Christian)
- **12** First game in UEFA Euro 2020, from Rome's Stadio Olympico
- **13** The Queen's official birthday
- **20** Summer solstice – start of astronomical summer, also known as Litha (neopagan) or Midsummer/Midsummer's Day
- **20** World Humanist Day
- **21** Father's Day
- **24** Traditional English midsummer, combined with Feast of St John the Baptist
- **24** 24th–28th: Glastonbury Festival

THE MOON

Names for June's full moon – Rose Moon, Dyad Moon

This is the month of the shortest, lightest and warmest nights. In the daytime the sun is high in the sky, and this means that the full moon – which must be opposite it in our sky in order to be full – stays lower and has a more golden tinge. We now view it through a greater slice of our atmosphere than we did at midwinter, and so it is softer and less bright until it climbs to its highest.

The medieval name for this month's moon is Rose Moon, reflecting the dog roses that are scrambling over hedgerows, their simple, pale pink petals catching the moonlight, as well as the abundance of roses wafting fragrantly from midnight gardens. It was also known as the Dyad Moon, 'dyad' meaning 'pair', and perhaps this is in reference to June being named after the Roman goddess of marriage, Juno, and being a month thought particularly favourable for weddings.

Moon phases

Full moon – *5th June, 19.12*

3rd quarter – *13th June, 06.24*

New moon – *21st June, 06.41*

1st quarter – *28th June, 08.16*

Moonrise and set

	Lowestoft		Dunquin		
	Rise	Set	Rise	Set	
1st	15.17	02.55	16.08	03.45	
2nd	16.42	03.14	17.33	04.04	
3rd	18.09	03.34	18.59	04.24	
4th	19.35	03.57	20.25	04.48	
5th	20.58	04.25	21.48	05.17	full moon
6th	22.13	05.02	23.02	05.54	
7th	23.15	05.49	–	06.42	
8th	–	06.48	00.04	07.41	
9th	00.03	07.55	00.51	08.48	
10th	00.39	09.07	01.27	10.00	
11th	01.05	10.19	01.54	11.12	
12th	01.26	11.30	02.15	12.22	
13th	01.44	12.39	02.32	13.31	3rd quarter
14th	01.59	13.47	02.48	14.38	
15th	02.13	14.54	03.02	15.45	
16th	02.28	16.02	03.17	16.53	
17th	02.43	17.12	03.34	18.02	
18th	03.02	18.23	03.52	19.13	
19th	03.24	19.34	04.15	20.23	
20th	03.53	20.43	04.45	21.32	
21st	04.31	21.46	05.24	22.35	new moon
22nd	05.21	22.40	06.14	23.28	
23rd	06.24	23.23	07.17	–	
24th	07.37	23.56	08.30	00.11	
25th	08.56	–	09.49	00.44	
26th	10.18	00.22	11.10	01.11	
27th	11.40	00.44	12.32	01.32	
28th	13.02	01.02	13.54	01.52	1st quarter
29th	14.25	01.21	15.16	02.10	
30th	15.49	01.39	16.39	02.29	

Where moonset times are before moonrise times, this is the setting of the previous night's moon.

Gardening by the moon

1st quarter to full moon: 1st–5th and 28th–30th. Sow crops that develop above ground. Plant seedlings and young plants.

Full moon to 3rd quarter: 5th–13th. Harvest crops for immediate eating. Harvest fruit.

3rd quarter to new moon: 13th–21st. Prune. Harvest for storage. Fertilise and mulch the soil.

New moon to 1st quarter: 21st–28th. Sow crops that develop below ground. Dig the soil.

June moon dates

5th – full moon: Vat Purnima. Hindu festival in which women pray for their husbands' prosperity. Purnima means 'full moon'.

5th and 21st – full moon and new moon: best fishing days. Some fishermen believe that fish bite best in the 45 minutes either side of moonrise and set on the full and new moons. So that would be 90 minutes from 03.40 and 20.13 on the 5th, and from 03.46 and 21.01 on the 21st (Lowestoft times).

21st – new moon in Cancer. This month's new moon is in Cancer, the sign governing home and family. Astrologers believe this is a good moment for beginning projects that will increase your domestic bliss. These plans will reach fruition around the next full moon in Cancer, on 30th December.

23rd – day after the calculated first sighting of the new crescent moon: the start of Tammuz. The Jewish month of Tammuz is named after the ancient Babylonian god of shepherds.

22nd (predicted) – day after the sighting of the new crescent moon: the start of Dhu'l-Qi'Dah. The beginning of the Islamic month Dhu'l-Qi'Dah, which means 'Master of Truce'. This is one of the Islamic year's four sacred months, and warfare is forbidden.

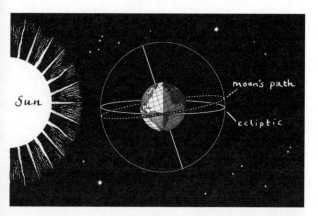

Why is the midsummer moon low, and the midwinter moon high?

The sun's apparent path through our sky throughout the year is called the ecliptic. The moon and planets also just about follow this line – the moon wavers slightly either side of it – but all move much faster, the moon travelling through all of the constellations of the zodiac that mark out its path each month, while the sun takes a year. At midsummer the northern hemisphere has tilted so that the ecliptic is at its highest point in our sky during the day, which means that as the earth turns and sends us into night, the ecliptic is at its lowest in our sky. A full moon only occurs when the moon is at the opposite point to the sun on the ecliptic, and so when we look at the midsummer moon it is low in our sky, and can appear larger and yellower than during the rest of the year. In December the opposite is true: our daytime is pointed towards a low ecliptic and a low sun, and our night-time towards a high, silvery bright moon.

THE SKY

At night

8th–9th Close approach of the moon, Jupiter and Saturn, visible from 00.30 in the southeast until lost in the dawn at 04.30, low in the southern sky.

13th Close approach of the moon and Mars, visible from 02:00 until lost in the dawn at 05:00, low in the southeastern sky.

By day

The summer solstice falls on 20th June at 22.44, when the North Pole is at its maximum tilt (23.44 degrees) towards the sun. The sun will be overhead at the tropic of Cancer (the northernmost latitude at which the sun can be directly overhead). The word solstice comes from the Latin *solstitium*, which means 'sun stopping', as the position on the horizon at which the sun rises and sets stops and reverses direction today.

The sun reaches an altitude of 62 degrees in the London sky and 58 degrees in the Glasgow sky at solar midday (13.00 BST/IST) on the solstice on 20th June.

Day length increases by 19m in Lowestoft, Suffolk, and by 19m in Dunquin, Republic of Ireland, until the 20th, and then decreases by 5m in Lowestoft, and by 5m in Dunquin. The 21st June is one second shorter, in both places.

Earliest sunrise (by a matter of seconds): 17th June, Lowestoft 04.29; 16th/17th June, Dunquin 05.20.

Latest sunset (by a matter of seconds): 24th June, Lowestoft 21.19, Dunquin 22.06.

Sunrise and set

	Lowestoft		*Dunquin*	
	Rise	Set	Rise	Set
1st	04.36	21.06	05.26	21.53
2nd	04.35	21.07	05.26	21.54
3rd	04.34	21.08	05.25	21.55
4th	04.33	21.09	05.24	21.56
5th	04.33	21.10	05.24	21.57
6th	04.32	21.11	05.23	21.58
7th	04.32	21.12	05.22	21.59
8th	04.31	21.13	05.22	22.00
9th	04.31	21.13	05.22	22.00
10th	04.30	21.14	05.21	22.01
11th	04.30	21.15	05.21	22.02
12th	04.30	21.16	05.21	22.02
13th	04.29	21.16	05.20	22.03
14th	04.29	21.17	05.20	22.04
15th	04.29	21.17	05.20	22.04
16th	04.29	21.18	05.20	22.04
17th	04.29	21.18	05.20	22.05
18th	04.29	21.18	05.20	22.05
19th	04.29	21.19	05.20	22.06
20th	04.29	21.19	05.20	22.06
21st	04.30	21.19	05.21	22.06
22nd	04.30	21.19	05.21	22.06
23rd	04.30	21.19	05.21	22.06
24th	04.31	21.19	05.21	22.06
25th	04.31	21.19	05.22	22.06
26th	04.31	21.19	05.22	22.06
27th	04.32	21.19	05.23	22.06
28th	04.33	21.19	05.23	22.06
29th	04.33	21.19	05.24	22.06
30th	04.34	21.18	05.25	22.05

J

THE SEA

Average sea temperature

Ayr:	11.9°C
Sunderland:	12.7°C
Dingle:	12.9°C
Dublin:	12.3°C
Aberystwyth:	13.0°C
Lowestoft:	13.8°C
Poole:	13.3°C
Newquay:	14.1°C

Spring and neap tides

The spring tides are the most extreme tides of the month, with the highest rises and falls, and the neap tides are the least extreme, with the smallest. Exact timings vary around the coast, but expect them around the following dates:

Spring tides: 6th–7th and 22nd–23rd

Neap tides: 14th–15th and 29th–30th

In the tide timetable opposite, spring tides are shown with an asterisk.

June tide timetable for Dover

For guidance on how to convert this for your local area, see page 8.

| | High water | | Low water | |
	Morning	Afternoon	Morning	Afternoon
1st	07.01	19.23	01.23	13.56
2nd	08.02	20.22	02.29	15.00
3rd	08.56	21.15	03.32	16.02
4th	09.45	22.04	04.36	17.02
5th	10.31	22.52	05.36	17.56
6th*	11.15	23.37	06.28	18.45
7th*	11.58	–	07.14	19.30
8th	00.21	12.42	07.56	20.12
9th	01.05	13.25	08.35	20.54
10th	01.49	14.10	09.13	21.34
11th	02.36	14.57	09.51	22.17
12th	03.26	15.47	10.32	23.05
13th	04.21	16.42	11.22	–
14th	05.22	17.43	00.02	12.25
15th	06.30	18.49	01.03	13.29
16th	07.34	19.49	02.02	14.28
17th	08.25	20.38	02.56	15.22
18th	09.08	21.19	03.46	16.11
19th	09.46	21.57	04.33	16.56
20th	10.23	22.34	05.18	17.38
21st	10.59	23.11	06.00	18.19
22nd*	11.35	23.49	06.42	19.01
23rd*	–	12.13	07.22	19.42
24th	00.28	12.54	08.02	20.23
25th	01.12	13.39	08.42	21.06
26th	01.59	14.29	09.24	21.53
27th	02.53	15.25	10.12	22.46
28th	03.56	16.27	11.07	23.46
29th	05.08	17.35	–	12.12
30th	06.24	18.47	11.51	13.20

NATURE

The hedgerow in June

It is the month of flowers in the hedgerow. All of the hedgerow roses are blooming their hearts out: dog rose and apple-scented sweet briar, as well as the downy rose, the burnet rose and the field rose. They scramble between bramble flowers, white bryony and blossoming honeysuckle up in the heights of the hedge. Between the petals in their elevated nest, the dormouse litter of four or five young has been born. They are pink, furless and blind, and are being carefully looked after by their mother.

Down at the hedgerow base, hoglets – baby hedgehogs – are being born this month and next. They are spineless and blind and the mother nurses them in her dug-out shelter. The badgers are out and about more, making day nests in the warm weather so that they can sleep above the ground. Cow parsley is still flowering and it has been joined by red campion, common orchids and foxgloves, which seem to be buzzing as bees crawl deep inside the flowers to reach their copious nectar, emerging smothered in pollen. Wild strawberries are ripening, too.

Hummingbird hawk moths and painted lady butterflies are also visiting the flowers. Hawthorn jewel beetles start feasting on hawthorn leaves and laying their eggs there. The larvae will hatch and make zigzag patterns beneath the surface. Small tortoiseshell larvae, having hatched this month on nettles, communally spin a web over themselves so that they can feed in safety.

HEDGEROW FLOWERS

goat's beard

common yarrow

red campion

J

meadow
cranesbill

foxglove

THE FLOWER GARDEN

June's flower garden picking prompts

Roses! And lots of them, mixed with alchemilla, scabious and hardy geraniums in a big, blowsy summer-border arrangement; a single peony flower floating in a bowl; a little scented posy of clove pinks, lavender and lemon thyme for a bedside table.

Jobs in the flower garden

- Get hold of some bulbs or plants of hardy cyclamen and plant them under trees or in the semi-shade of shrubs, where nothing else will grow. They will bloom in autumn, their diminutive lavender and pale pink flowers brightening up dull corners. This is also the time to plant autumn crocuses in the same sorts of spots.
- Sow biennials for flowering next spring and summer: wallflowers, honesty, foxgloves, night-scented stock, sweet rocket, sweet william and Iceland poppy all flower in their second year of life, and so should be started into growth now and planted out in August in the spot where they are to flower next year.
- Now that primulas have finished flowering, you can lift and divide them to spread them around your garden and give you a flower-strewn patch next spring. Get your garden fork under a clump and carefully lever it up, then use your hands to gently pull apart the rosettes of leaves, making sure each comes with a bit of root attached. Plant in their new spots and water in straight away. Keep watering as they establish.

CHARM OF THE MONTH

Midsummer cushions

In medieval times, 'midsummer' was a loose community celebration that ran between St John the Baptist's Eve on 23rd June to St Peter's Day on 29th June. (You will note that actual midsummer's day is missed out completely, as 24th June, the Feast of St John the Baptist, was traditionally considered midsummer.) The festivities centred around fires, flowers and feasting. Doors were hung with birch, fennel, lilies and wild flowers, and in the evenings bonfires and lamps would be lit outside shops and houses, food and drink laid out on tables, and neighbours invited to partake.

Midsummer cushions were the children's contribution to the floral bounty of what must have been a magical time. They were made in various ways – some from a board smeared with clay or mud and then stuck all over with petals, and some made from an actual cushion that was threaded with wild flowers. The Northamptonshire poet John Clare reported that children would take a piece of 'greensward', or turf, and stick it with meadow flowers to place in their cottages in a celebration of the natural abundance of this golden moment in the year. He entitled one of his books of poetry *The Midsummer Cushion*, and the custom has been revived in his native village of Helpston, where local children make midsummer cushions to decorate his grave on the weekend closest to his birthday on 13th July.

THE KITCHEN GARDEN

Spring's direct sowings will now need thinning out to allow the vegetables space to mature. Thin carrots in the evening when the carrot fly is less prevalent. Make a second sowing of French beans and courgettes this month, to see you right through to late summer. Sweetcorn should be planted out in blocks, with each plant 30cm or so apart, to aid wind pollination. Keep up with your successional sowing of carrots, beetroot, radishes, spring onions and lettuce leaves. If you started cutting your asparagus early, you may have to stop this month and let the spears turn ferny – harvest for no longer than eight weeks.

Sowing and planting crops

Fruit/veg	Sow under cover	Sow direct	Plant
Aubergines			✓
Courgettes	✓	✓	✓
Summer squash	✓	✓	✓
Pumpkins			✓
Winter squash			✓
Cucumbers		✓	✓
Sweetcorn		✓	✓
Florence fennel		✓	✓
French beans		✓	✓
Runner beans		✓	✓
Summer and autumn cabbages			✓
Winter cabbages			✓
Kohlrabi		✓	✓
Sprouting broccoli		✓	✓
Calabrese		✓	✓
Kale		✓	
Brussels sprouts			✓
Celeriac			✓
Leeks			✓
Lettuces	✓	✓	✓

Fruit/veg	Sow under cover	Sow direct	Plant
Salad leaves	✓	✓	✓
Chicory and radicchio			✓
Spring onions		✓	
Spinach and Swiss chard		✓	
Beetroot		✓	
Chives		✓	
Parsley		✓	
Dill		✓	
Basil	✓	✓	
Fennel (leaf)		✓	
Carrots		✓	
Turnips		✓	
Radishes		✓	
Runner beans		✓	
French beans	✓	✓	

J

THE KITCHEN

Sauce of the month – mulato chilli barbecue sauce
This makes a sweet and smoky but not too fiery sauce
for marinating chicken overnight ahead of grilling on the
barbecue, or for dipping. Remove the seeds and stalks from
four mulato chillies (dried poblanos, which you can find
in specialist online delis) and put them into a dry pan and
dry fry them for a minute or two. Put them into a bowl and
cover with boiling water, then leave them to soak for at least
30 minutes. Meanwhile, finely dice an onion and cook until
soft and translucent in olive oil. Add six finely chopped or
crushed cloves of garlic and cook for a few more minutes, then
add 150g tomato purée and cook until warmed through and
bubbling. Tip this mixture into a food processor and add the
drained chillies – reserving the soaking liquid for later – along
with 2 tablespoons muscovado sugar, half a teaspoon of salt,
a pinch of ground cloves and half a teaspoon chipotle chilli
flakes. Purée to a paste, adding the reserved chilli soaking
water as needed to bring it to a sauce consistency. If you want a
smoother sauce, you can push it through a sieve before serving.
Add salt and pepper and more chipotle to taste.

In season
Vegetables: broad beans, globe artichokes, asparagus, French
beans, peas, lettuces, radishes, Florence fennel, carrots,
beetroot, new potatoes, Swiss chard, spinach, turnips,
cauliflowers, calabrese, kohlrabi, garlic, onions
Herbs: chives, basil, mint, dill, marjoram, thyme, oregano
Fruit: strawberries, raspberries, cherries, apricots, gooseberries,
blackcurrants, white currants, redcurrants
Dairy: ewe's curd, ricotta, chèvre
Fish: crab, mackerel, sardines

RECIPES

Mini strawberry *rumtopf*

Rumtopf, meaning 'rum pot', is a German dessert involving a
method of preserving the many fruits of the year into winter.
It is traditionally made in a large stoneware crock with a lid,
and is begun around June when the strawberries ripen, and
then layers are added as the season goes on, right through to
October. It can, therefore, contain layers of apricots, cherries,
peaches, plums, redcurrants, raspberries, blackberries, figs,
apples, pears and grapes. The recipe given here is for a smaller,
strawberry version, assembled in a 1-litre Kilner jar and put
away in June to provide midwinter strawberries. But if you
have a big enough pot, there is nothing to stop you layering
all summer long, using the proportions given here.

Makes 1 litre
Ingredients
500g strawberries
250g golden caster sugar
About 350ml overproof dark rum

Method

Wash and hull the strawberries. Sprinkle a layer of sugar
in the bottom of a sterilisd 1-litre Kilner jar. Add a layer of
strawberries, followed by sugar, and continue alternating layers
of strawberries and sugar until all is used up. Leave for an hour,
and then pour the rum over it. Place a piece of clingfilm over
the surface of the mixture, then seal the jar or pot. (If you are
using a large pot and will be adding more fruit later, unseal the
pot at the time, remove the clingfilm, add the fruit, sugar and
rum, and re-cover as before. Apples, pears and peaches should
be peeled before they go in, but everything else can go in with
the skin on, as long as it is clean and the stones and stems

have been removed.) Store somewhere cool and dark. The last
additions to the pot should have been in for at least 4 weeks
before the pot is opened and the fruit spooned over ice cream
or pavlova.

Midsummer cushion cakes for the solstice

It is sad that the tradition for making midsummer cushions has
all but died out (see page 133), but you can bring it back in your
own kitchen by dotting a tapestry of edible flowers over little
summer-scented cakes.

Makes 12 fairy cakes
Ingredients
150g softened butter
150g golden caster sugar
Seeds of 1 vanilla pod
½ teaspoon rosewater
1 head of lavender, broken up (optional)
Zest of 1 lemon
Handful of rose petals (optional)
3 eggs
150g self-raising flour
1 teaspoon baking powder
Pinch of salt

For icing
250g mascarpone
1 tablespoon runny honey
Zest and juice of 1 lemon

For decoration

Petals from edible flowers, such as rose, borage, jasmine, carnation, cornflower, pot marigold and lavender

Handful of wild strawberries, if you can find them – or a few fresh strawberries, chopped

Method

To make the cakes, first preheat the oven to 190°C, Gas Mark 5, and fill a cake tray with paper cake cups. Cream the butter and the sugar together until fluffy and pale. Add the vanilla seeds, rosewater, lavender head (if using), the lemon zest and the rose petals (if using). Stir well, then beat in the eggs one at a time. Sift the flour and baking powder into the mixture and add the salt, then stir until everything is combined. Spoon the batter into the paper cases so they are about one-third full (you can do a second tray if you have leftover mixture).

Bake for 12–15 minutes, or until the top of each cake bounces back when lightly pressed. Remove from the oven and cool on a wire rack.

To make the icing, mix the mascarpone with the honey and the lemon zest, adding a little lemon juice if you need it to loosen it. When the cakes are completely cool, ice them with the mascarpone mixture, and then decorate with the edible petals and strawberries.

A SONG FOR JUNE'S FULL MOON

'Lament to the Moon'
Traditional, arr. Richard Barnard

This is an old Irish song that portrays the moon as comforting the broken-hearted, or at least illuminating them romantically. There may be roses and nightingales and a perfect silvery moon, but none of this will bring back a long-lost lover.

As I went on my way at the close of the day
About the beginning of June.
It was there in a glade that I saw a fair maid
As she sang her lament to the moon.

Roll along silvery moon, guide the traveller's way
While the nightingale sings its sweet tune.
But I'll never away with my true love to stray
By the light of the silvery moon.

My lover was brave as the hart on the hill
His arms they were brawny and strong.
So kind, so sincere, and he loved me so dear
As he sang me his old shanty songs.

But now he is gone, never more to return
Cut down like a rose in full bloom.
As he silently sleeps I am left here to weep
By the light of the silvery moon.

July

- **11** Wimbledon Women's Final
- **12** Wimbledon Men's Final
- **12** UEFA Euro 2020 Final, from Wembley Stadium, London
- **12** Battle of the Boyne commemoration, Northern Ireland
- **13** Battle of the Boyne bank holiday, Northern Ireland
- **14** Sea Sunday (Christian)
- **15** St Swithin's Day (Christian, traditional)
- **23** Birthday of Haile Selassie (Rastafarian)
- **28** 28th July–2nd August: Hajj (Muslim pilgrimage to Mecca)
- **30** Tisha B'Av (Jewish day of mourning)

THE MOON

Names for July's full moon – Wyrt Moon, Mead Moon

July is lush and green. The trees have lost their youthful, lime green tinges and settled into their mid-green high summer coats. The first flush of flowers has passed but their fruits have not yet ripened. Greenery is in the ascendant beneath July's full moon. *Wyrt* is an Old English word for 'herbs', and the medieval name Wyrt Moon for July's full moon reflects the fact that while little has ripened yet, greenery and herbs are plentiful. This is also the time beekeepers take their first honey of the year, and so the making of mead – a fermented honey drink – could begin, an important pastime in medieval Britain. Perhaps this sweet intoxicating drink would be made by the helpful light of the full moon if chores had stacked up, hence the name Mead Moon.

Moon phases

Full moon – *5th July, 04.44*

3rd quarter – *12th July, 23.29*

New moon – *20th July, 17.33*

1st quarter – *27th July, 12.33*

Moonrise and set

	Lowestoft		*Dunquin*		
	Rise	Set	Rise	Set	
1st	17.13	02.00	18.03	02.50	
2nd	18.36	02.25	19.25	03.16	
3rd	19.53	02.57	20.42	03.49	
4th	21.01	03.38	21.49	04.31	
5th	21.55	04.32	22.43	05.25	full moon
6th	22.36	05.35	23.24	06.29	
7th	23.06	06.46	23.55	07.39	
8th	23.30	07.59	–	08.52	
9th	23.49	09.12	00.18	10.04	
10th	–	10.23	00.37	11.14	
11th	00.05	11.32	00.54	12.23	
12th	00.19	12.39	01.09	13.30	3rd quarter
13th	00.34	13.47	01.23	14.38	
14th	00.49	14.55	01.39	15.46	
15th	01.06	16.05	01.56	16.55	
16th	01.26	17.16	02.17	18.06	
17th	01.52	18.26	02.43	19.16	
18th	02.26	19.33	03.18	20.22	
19th	03.11	20.31	04.04	21.20	
20th	04.09	21.19	05.02	22.07	new moon
21st	05.20	21.56	06.13	22.45	
22nd	06.39	22.25	07.32	23.14	
23rd	08.02	22.49	08.55	23.58	
24th	09.26	23.09	10.19	23.58	
25th	10.50	23.27	11.42	–	
26th	12.13	23.45	13.05	00.17	
27th	13.36	–	14.27	00.35	1st quarter
28th	14.59	00.05	15.50	00.56	
29th	16.21	00.28	17.11	01.19	
30th	17.39	00.57	18.29	01.49	
31st	18.49	01.34	19.38	02.26	

Where moonset times are before moonrise times, this is the setting of the previous night's moon.

Gardening by the moon

1st quarter to full moon: 1st–5th and 27th–31st. Sow crops that develop above ground. Plant seedlings and young plants.

Full moon to 3rd quarter: 5th–12th. Harvest crops for immediate eating. Harvest fruit.

3rd quarter to new moon: 12th–20th. Prune. Harvest for storage. Fertilise and mulch the soil.

New moon to 1st quarter: 20th–27th. Sow crops that develop below ground. Dig the soil.

July moon dates

5th – full moon: Asalha Puja/Dharma Day. The day upon which Buddhists commemorate Buddha's first sermon.

5th – full moon: Guru Purnima. Hindu festival and the day devotees offer *puja* (worship) to their gurus.

5th and 20th – full moon and new moon: best fishing days. Some fishermen believe that fish bite best in the 45 minutes either side of moonrise and set on the full and new moons. So that would be 90 minutes from 03.47 and 21.10 on the 5th, and from 03.24 and 20.34 on the 20th (Lowestoft times).

20th – new moon in Cancer. This month's new moon is still in Cancer, the sign governing home and family. Astrologers believe this is a good moment for beginning projects that will increase your domestic bliss. These plans will reach fruition around the next full moon in Cancer, on 30th December.

22nd – day after the calculated first sighting of the new crescent moon: the start of Av. This month is the anniversary of some of the darkest moments in Jewish history. Tisha B'Av ('the 9th of Av') is considered the saddest day in the Jewish calendar and is a day of fasting and remembrance.

22nd (predicted) – day after the sighting of the new crescent moon: the start of Dhu'l-Hijjah. This is one of the four sacred months of Islam. The name means 'month of pilgrimage', and on the 9th, 10th and 11th of the month Muslims visit Mecca.

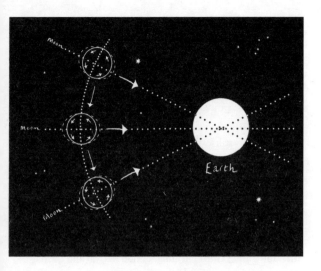

Why do we see only one side of the moon?

This is down to a phenomenon known as 'tidal locking'. The moon was created when a vast, planet-sized body ploughed into earth 4.5 billion years ago. The moon was much closer to earth then, and so the pull of earth's gravity was much stronger on it, and – just as our tides are pulled about by the gravity of the moon – the solid mass of the moon was pulled by the earth's gravity into a slightly oval shape. As the moon spun around on its axis, this bulge at first swung repeatedly out of alignment with earth, but earth repeatedly pulled it back into line until finally it was locked in place. This process took around ten million years, and since then the moon has made exactly one rotation on its axis for every orbit it makes of the earth, and so we are always looking at one side of it.

THE SKY

At night

6th Close approach of the moon, Jupiter and Saturn, visible from 00.30 in the southeast until setting in the southwest at 05.00. The group will reach maximum altitude of 17 degrees at 02.00.

12th Close approach of the moon and Mars, visible from midnight until lost in the dawn at 05.00, low in the southeastern sky.

14th Jupiter is at opposition and so will be at its brightest and largest tonight. Visible from 21.00 in the southeast and reaching an altitude of 16 degrees at midnight in the south before setting in the southwest at 05.00. It will be visible and bright for several weeks either side of this.

17th Close approach of the moon and Venus, visible low in the northeast sky from about 03.00 until lost in the dawn at an altitude of 25 degrees at 05.00.

By day

Aphelion is the point in the year when the earth is farthest from the sun. This falls on 4th July at 12.34, when the sun will be 152,095,295km away (compare with perihelion on 5th January, see page 16).

The sun reaches an altitude of 59 degrees in the London sky and 50 degrees in the Glasgow sky at solar midday (13.00 BST/IST) on 21st July.

Day length decreases by 1h 10m in Lowestoft, Suffolk, and by 1h 9m in Dunquin, Republic of Ireland.

Earliest sunrise (by a matter of seconds): 1st July, Lowestoft 04.34, Dunquin 05.25.

Latest sunset (by a matter of seconds): 1st July, Lowestoft 21.18, Dunquin 22.05.

Sunrise and set

	Lowestoft		*Dunquin*	
	Rise	Set	Rise	Set
1st	04.34	21.18	05.25	22.05
2nd	04.35	21.18	05.26	22.05
3rd	04.36	21.17	05.27	22.04
4th	04.37	21.17	05.28	22.04
5th	04.38	21.16	05.29	22.03
6th	04.39	21.16	05.29	22.02
7th	04.40	21.15	05.30	22.02
8th	04.41	21.14	05.31	22.01
9th	04.42	21.13	05.32	22.00
10th	04.43	21.13	05.33	22.00
11th	04.44	21.12	05.34	21.59
12th	04.45	21.11	05.36	21.58
13th	04.46	21.10	05.37	21.57
14th	04.47	21.09	05.38	21.56
15th	04.49	21.08	05.39	21.55
16th	04.50	21.07	05.40	21.54
17th	04.51	21.05	05.42	21.53
18th	04.52	21.04	05.43	21.51
19th	04.54	21.03	05.44	21.50
20th	04.55	21.02	05.46	21.49
21st	04.57	21.00	05.47	21.48
22nd	04.58	20.59	05.48	21.46
23rd	04.59	20.58	05.50	21.45
24th	05.01	20.56	05.51	21.44
25th	05.02	20.55	05.53	21.42
26th	05.04	20.53	05.54	21.41
27th	05.05	20.52	05.56	21.39
28th	05.07	20.50	05.57	21.38
29th	05.08	20.49	05.59	21.36
30th	05.10	20.47	06.00	21.34
31st	05.11	20.45	06.02	21.33

J

THE SEA

Average sea temperature

Ayr:	13.7°C
Sunderland:	15.1°C
Dingle:	14.8°C
Dublin:	14.1°C
Aberystwyth:	14.8°C
Lowestoft:	15.6°C
Poole:	15.2°C
Newquay:	16.4°C

Spring and neap tides

The spring tides are the most extreme tides of the month, with the highest rises and falls, and the neap tides are the least extreme, with the smallest. Exact timings vary around the coast, but expect them around the following dates:

Spring tides: 6th–7th and 23rd–24th

Neap tides: 14th–15th and 29th–30th

In the tide timetable opposite, spring tides are shown with an asterisk.

July tide timetable for Dover

For guidance on how to convert this for your local area, see page 8.

| | High water | | Low water | |
	Morning	Afternoon	Morning	Afternoon
1st	07.32	19.54	01.56	14.26
2nd	08.33	20.56	03.01	15.32
3rd	09.28	21.52	04.09	16.38
4th	10.19	22.43	05.16	17.38
5th	11.05	23.29	06.12	18.31
6th*	11.47	–	07.00	19.18
7th*	00.12	12.29	07.43	20.01
8th	00.53	13.10	08.21	20.40
9th	01.33	13.50	08.56	21.16
10th	02.14	14.31	09.26	21.49
11th	02.56	15.12	09.53	22.21
12th	03.41	15.56	10.27	23.00
13th	04.32	16.46	11.11	23.52
14th	05.31	17.46	–	12.10
15th	06.34	18.49	00.56	13.25
16th	07.35	19.49	02.03	14.33
17th	08.27	20.41	03.04	15.33
18th	09.14	21.28	04.00	16.25
19th	09.58	22.12	04.51	17.14
20th	10.39	22.55	05.39	18.01
21st	11.20	23.37	06.26	18.48
22nd	–	12.01	07.12	19.34
23rd*	00.19	12.44	07.56	20.19
24th*	01.02	13.28	08.38	21.02
25th	01.48	14.14	09.18	21.45
26th	02.36	15.04	10.00	22.30
27th	03.30	15.59	10.46	23.20
28th	04.32	17.01	11.40	–
29th	05.45	18.13	00.19	12.46
30th	07.05	19.33	01.26	13.57
31st	08.17	20.47	02.37	15.11

NATURE

The hedgerow in July

The bramble is still flowering, but the first green fruits are starting to form, and they are joined now by hedge bindweed and the aptly named traveller's joy, the cheerful yellow wild clematis that changes its common name as the year goes on (it will be 'old man's beard' by November). Hedge parsley and wild carrot come into flower this month, both of them resembling cow parsley (though the hedge parsley is a pinker version) and just as attractive to insects who flock to them. All the insects of the hedgerow are busy getting their fill. Speckled wood butterfly, hoverfly, gatekeeper butterfly, Jersey tiger moth, red-tailed bumblebee, seven-spotted ladybird, buff-tailed bumblebee, honeybee, leafcutter bee, ringlet butterfly, painted lady butterfly, green bottle fly, peacock butterfly and small tortoiseshell butterfly might be seen. There are plenty of creatures feasting on the greenery, too, and spotted longhorn beetles are feeding on cow parsley and hawthorn.

July sees the first good crop of fruits, which are a great boon to the residents of the hedgerow. The cherry plums and wild cherries have started to ripen, along with more wild strawberries. Beneath the ground, attached to the roots of hazels, summer truffles have formed and may be dug up by foraging mammals. Hoglets (baby hedgehogs) start to go on foraging trips with their mother. About two weeks later they will set out on their own. Dormouse babies start to forage with their mother when they are a few weeks old. The creatures' diet has switched from flowers to buds and insects. A common lizard may emerge from the shelter of the hedgerow and take up a position on a well-placed stone to bask in the warmth of the sun.

THE FLOWER GARDEN

July's flower garden picking prompts

Sweet peas, in vases and glasses all over your house – pick them and they will make more; a single stem of a lily in an elegant narrow-necked vase on a desk; a cloud of sweet rocket and poppies.

Jobs in the flower garden

- Nerines are bulbs that produce their vibrant, almost too pink flowers in autumn, a season not known for its pinks. This is the time to plant them in your sunniest spot. The bulbs need to really bake each summer, and if they get this they will bulk up over time to become quite spectacular.
- You will prolong and increase the flowering of everything if you spend some time on two little jobs: deadheading and feeding. Deadheading means snipping off the flowers that have gone over, to fool your plants into producing more, though hanging baskets will benefit from a proper trim all over now, too. And to feed, buy an organic feed high in potash (such as tomato feed) and add a little to the watering can at least once a week.
- Annual cut flowers such as calendula, cornflower, love-in-a-mist and poppy are starting to run to seed. On a dry day, collect up the seed, label it and store it away for sowing in autumn or next spring. Place seeds in labelled paper bags and pop the bags into an airtight container with a couple of handfuls of rice in the base, to absorb any moisture.

J

BEES

common carder bee

red-tailed bumblebee

white-tailed bumblebee

tree bumblebee

honey bee

CHARM OF THE MONTH

Bees

Though you can't pop a bee into your pocket to cling to in times of worry (ouch), they have traditionally had so many lucky associations that they can surely count as charms, albeit living, breathing, honey-making ones. A bee landing on you is very lucky, and one flying into your house will bring luck or a visitor, as long as you let it find its own way out naturally. Their lucky symbolism must be connected to their great importance in creating such a vital and delicious source of food. There are also several superstitions relating to their sensitive nature and the perils of treating them badly, presumably stemming from their propensity to fly away or die if they don't find conditions exactly to their liking. Bees will not stay in an argumentative household, and they particularly object to swearing. A hive should never be owned by one person; indeed, it is at its luckiest when owned by an unmarried man and an unmarried woman. And the hive needs to be kept informed – if a daughter of the household is to be married, you must whisper it to the bees. You must also do this when a member of the household dies, as the bees must be allowed to mourn or they will fly away. Needless to say, to kill a bee will bring terrible luck.

J

THE KITCHEN GARDEN

This is the moment to start sowing Oriental leaves for autumn and winter: try mizuna, mibuna and pak choi, sown direct into the ground or into modules to plant out next month. It is a time of changeover in the kitchen garden. If you haven't already harvested broad beans, garlic and onions, do so this month, and you will create space for winter vegetables such as Brussels sprouts, winter cabbages and purple sprouting broccoli. As you plant these brassicas you will need to construct a brassica frame around them covered in a fine mesh to prevent them from being attacked by cabbage white butterflies and pigeons. Lift garlic, onions and shallots during dry, sunny weather and lay them on the ground to dry out in the sun, to help them store well. Feed tomatoes at least once a week now with an organic liquid to help their fruits develop. You'll also need to feed sweet peppers, winter squash and all other fruit-producing vegetables, though none are quite as greedy as tomatoes. This may be the time to 'stop' tomatoes, nipping out the tips after five trusses of fruit have formed. New fruits formed after this may not have time to ripen before the end of summer, and they will slow the ripening of those trusses already on the plant. Stop cutting asparagus this month, eight weeks after starting, and let the spears turn ferny.

Sowing and planting crops

Fruit/veg	Sow under cover	Sow direct	Plant
Florence fennel		✓	
French beans		✓	✓
Spring cabbages	✓	✓	
Winter cabbages			✓
Kohlrabi		✓	
Calabrese		✓	
Kale	✓	✓	
Brussels sprouts			✓
Leeks			✓

Fruit/veg	Sow under cover	Sow direct	Plant
Lettuces	✓	✓	✓
Salad leaves	✓	✓	✓
Chicory and radicchio			✓
Spring onions		✓	
Oriental leaves	✓	✓	✓
Radishes	✓	✓	✓
Spinach and Swiss chard		✓	
Beetroot		✓	
Basil	✓	✓	
Carrots		✓	
Turnips		✓	
Radishes		✓	
French beans		✓	✓
Peas	✓	✓	✓

J

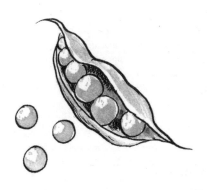

THE KITCHEN

Sauce of the month – classic pesto

Under the Wyrt ('herb') Moon, it must be time to make this well-loved herb sauce. Freshly made pesto eaten within an hour of being made is a world away from the stuff in jars. It is the flavour of summer and well worth preparing while the basil is flowing freely. It's really quick, too. While it's obviously great on pasta, you can also just blob it around the side of salads, omelettes and roasted veg. Put a pinch of salt and a clove of garlic into a pestle and mortar and pound to a paste, then add 60g toasted pine nuts and grind them, too. Next pound in a large handful of basil leaves. Add 60g finely grated Parmesan cheese and some extra virgin olive oil, and work into a thick paste. Squeeze a little lemon juice in to freshen and brighten it, then add more olive oil to the desired consistency. Season with salt and pepper if needed. You can mess about with this formula depending on the season and your taste – try toasted hazelnuts, walnuts or almonds instead of pine nuts; hard goat's cheese, Cheddar or Pecorino instead of Parmesan; and parsley, chervil, tarragon, coriander, rocket, blanched nettles or wild garlic instead of basil.

In season

Vegetables: new potatoes, young carrots, beetroot, salad leaves, Florence fennel, asparagus, globe artichokes, peas, mangetouts, spring onions, onions, shallots, lettuces, runner beans, French beans, celery, rocket, calabrese, courgettes, the last of the broad beans. Samphire's short season has begun.

Herbs: mint, basil, dill, chives, marjoram, thyme, oregano, calendula flowers, courgette flowers, nasturtium flowers

Fruit: apricots, peaches, early plums, nectarines, cherries, raspberries, currants, gooseberries, blueberries, strawberries, and the first plums and blackberries

Dairy: ewe's curd, ricotta, chèvre

Fish: sea bass, mackerel, sardine, crab

RECIPES

Ricotta and herb drop scones

Savoury, herby pancakes to further celebrate the Wyrt Moon and its association with herbs. Perfect with crispy bacon and poached eggs.

Makes about 12 small pancakes, to serve 4
Ingredients
2 eggs, separated
100g plain flour
1 teaspoon baking powder
Pinch of salt
150ml whole milk
150g ricotta
50g Parmesan, grated
Large handful of finely chopped herbs, such as basil, chives, dill, oregano, thyme, parsley
50g butter

Method

In a large bowl, whisk the two egg whites until the firm peak stage – when you lift the whisk out, the whisked egg forms a peak that holds but bends back on itself. Put the flour, baking powder and salt in another bowl and make a well in the centre, then add a little of the milk and the two egg yolks to the well. Start to carefully whisk, including a little more of the flour at each turn, and adding more of the milk as it thickens, until all the flour is incorporated. Whisk in the ricotta, Parmesan and herbs, and then carefully fold in the whisked egg whites.

Heat a little butter in a frying pan and add spoonfuls of the mixture. Fry them until small bubbles appear and solidify on the surface, and then flip them over and fry for a minute more.

Serve them as they come out of the pan, or keep the cooked pancakes warm in a low oven while you make the rest. They will lose a little of their fluffiness and volume but will still be good. Serve with poached eggs and crispy bacon.

Heg peg dump

The 20th July is St Margaret's Day, who is the patron saint of safe childbirth because, when she was swallowed by a dragon, a cross appeared in her hand, splitting open the dragon's belly and allowing her to step out unharmed. Heg peg dump is a suet pudding, or dumpling, that was traditionally eaten in her honour on this day in Gloucestershire. Heg is for hedgerow, as it is made from hedgerow plums, Peg is the nickname for Margaret, and dump is for dumpling. Its original and true form is a suet-crust pudding, which needs to be steamed for up to three hours. This recipe is for a simpler, cobbler-like arrangement that makes use of the same components but involves dumplings (albeit ones flavoured with vanilla) – so we can still call it a heg peg dump of sorts. It is lovely served piping hot, with cold thick cream or vanilla ice cream.

Serves 6

Ingredients

For the fruit

800g wild plums (other plums will do), quartered, stones removed

4 eating apples, peeled, cored and sliced

75g golden caster sugar

Zest and juice of 1 lemon

For the dumplings

225g self-raising flour

Pinch of salt

110g fridge-cold butter

1 vanilla pod

Zest of 1 lemon

2 tablespoons golden caster sugar

Method

To prepare the fruit, preheat the oven to 190°C, Gas Mark 5.
Put the fruit ingredients into a pan with a few tablespoons of
water. Bring to the boil, then reduce the heat and simmer gently,
adding a little more water if it needs it and stirring until the
fruit is collapsed and the plums have released lots of their own
juices. Tip into an ovenproof dish.

To make the dumplings, put the flour and salt in a large
bowl, and grate in the cold butter. Split the vanilla pod,
and scrape in the vanilla seeds; add the lemon zest. Rub
in with your fingertips until the mixture resembles coarse
breadcrumbs. Stir in the sugar, then add just enough water to
make a thick dough. Take tablespoonfuls of mixture and float
them on top of the fruit until all of the dumpling mixture is
used up. Bake for 20–25 minutes, or until the dumplings are
risen and slightly browned on top. Serve hot with cold double
cream or vanilla ice cream.

A SONG FOR JULY'S FULL MOON

'The Man in the Moon'
Traditional, arr. Richard Barnard

This jaunty old Sussex dance tune takes as its subject the poor man in the moon himself, who, for all his grandeur and beauty, must get a bit lonesome up there on his own.

The man in the moon seems to lead a queer life
With no one around him, not even a wife;
No friends to console him, no children to kiss,
No chance of his joining a party like this.
He changes his lodgings each quarter anew
After leaving a circus, a crescent will do
If he rents in these quarters so fast going by
I imagine his rent is uncommonly high,
But he's used to the high life, all circles agree,
For none move in circles as high up as he.
Though nobles go up in their royal balloon,
They can't get to meet him, the man in the moon.

It is said that some people are moonstruck, we find,
And the man in the moon could be out of his mind.
But it can't be for love, for he's quite on his own,
No lovers to meet him by moonlight alone.
It can't be ambition, for rivals he's none,
At least he is only eclipsed by the sun,
But when drinking, I say, he is seldom surpassed,
For he always looks best when he's seen through a glass.
Oh, the man in the moon a new light on us throws,
He's a man we all talk of but nobody knows.
And though a high subject, I'm getting in tune,
I'll just sing a song for the man in the moon.

J

August

- **1** Lammas (Christian) and Lughnasadh (pagan/neopagan)

- **3** August bank holiday, Scotland, Republic of Ireland

- **7** 7th–31st: Edinburgh Festival

- **12** The Glorious Twelfth – grouse-shooting season begins

- **12** Krishna Janmashtami – Krishna's birthday (Hindu)

- **15** The Assumption of Mary (Christian)

- **20** Al Hijra – Islamic New Year, beginning of Islamic year 1442 (Muslim)

- **29** 29th–31st: Notting Hill Carnival, London

- **31** Summer bank holiday, England, Wales, Northern Ireland

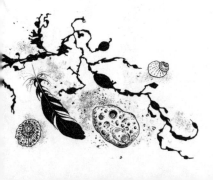

THE MOON

Names for August's full moon – Grain Moon, Lynx Moon

Spend time in the countryside this month and it is easy to see why the name Grain Moon was once used for August's full moon. This is the moment that fields of wheat are ripening to soft gold, with warm breezes rippling them in the moonlight. Harvest time has begun. The name Lynx Moon has not stood the test of time in the same way, namely because lynxes were driven out of Britain 1,300 years ago. It is a bit of a mystery as to why lynxes might have been so noticeable this month to warrant calling the moon after them – however, they do hunt at night, and August might have been a time when there were more of them around, as the cubs born in spring grew large enough to hunt. A more likely explanation might be that the word lynx is derived from the Middle English word *leuk*, meaning 'light', or 'brightness', given to lynxes because of their pale yellow, reflective eyes. 'Lynx' might therefore have been a reference to the brightness of the moon itself (perhaps as a result of the 'moon illusion', which is often more noticeable in late summer – see page 209) rather than because of the presence of this very shy animal.

Moon phases

Full moon – *3rd August, 15.59*

3rd quarter – *11th August, 16.45*

New moon – *19th August, 02.42*

1st quarter – *25th August, 17.58*

Moonrise and set

	Lowestoft		*Dunquin*		
	Rise	Set	Rise	Set	
1st	19.47	02.22	20.36	03.15	
2nd	20.32	03.21	21.21	04.14	
3rd	21.06	04.29	21.55	05.22	full moon
4th	21.32	06.54	22.21	06.34	
5th	21.53	06.54	22.41	07.47	
6th	22.10	08.06	22.59	08.58	
7th	22.25	09.16	23.14	10.08	
8th	22.39	10.25	23.29	11.16	
9th	22.54	11.32	23.44	12.23	
10th	23.10	12.40	–	13.31	
11th	23.28	13.49	00.00	14.39	3rd quarter
12th	23.51	14.59	00.19	15.49	
13th	–	16.09	00.42	16.58	
14th	00.21	17.16	01.12	18.05	
15th	01.00	18.18	01.52	19.07	
16th	01.52	19.10	02.45	19.59	
17th	02.57	19.52	03.50	20.41	
18th	04.14	20.25	05.07	21.14	
19th	05.38	20.51	06.31	21.40	new moon
20th	07.04	21.13	07.57	22.02	
21st	08.31	21.32	09.23	22.21	
22nd	09.57	21.50	10.49	22.40	
23rd	11.22	22.10	12.14	23.00	
24th	12.47	22.32	13.39	23.23	
25th	14.11	22.59	15.01	23.50	1st quarter
26th	15.30	23.33	16.20	–	
27th	16.43	–	17.32	00.25	
28th	17.44	00.17	18.32	01.10	
29th	18.32	01.12	19.20	02.05	
30th	19.08	02.17	19.56	03.10	
31st	19.36	03.27	20.24	04.20	

Where moonset times are before moonrise times, this is the setting of
the previous night's moon.

Gardening by the moon

1st quarter to full moon: 1st–3rd and 25th–31st. Sow crops that develop above ground. Plant seedlings and young plants.

Full moon to 3rd quarter: 3rd–11th. Harvest crops for immediate eating. Harvest fruit.

3rd quarter to new moon: 11th–19th. Prune. Harvest for storage. Fertilise and mulch the soil.

New moon to 1st quarter: 19th–25th. Sow crops that develop below ground. Dig the soil.

August moon dates

3rd – full moon: Raksha bandhan. Hindu full moon festival celebrating the bond between brothers and sisters.

3rd and 19th – full moon and new moon: best fishing days. Some fishermen believe that fish bite best in the 45 minutes either side of moonrise and set on the full and new moons. So that would be 90 minutes from 03.44 and 20.21 on the 3rd, and from 04.53 and 20.06 on the 19th (Lowestoft times).

19th – new moon in Leo. This month's new moon is in confident and energetic Leo – astrologers believe this is a time for planning projects involving fun and self-promotion. Plans made now will come to fruition around the next full moon in Leo, on 28th January 2021.

20th (predicted) – day after sighting of new crescent moon: the start of Muharram. This is the second holiest month in the Islamic year, after Ramadan. Muharram means 'sacred' or 'forbidden' – all fighting is forbidden this month.

21st – day after calculated first sighting of new crescent moon: the start of Elul. The name for the Jewish month Elul may be related to the verb for 'search' in Aramaic. Elul is a month for searching one's heart in preparation for the day of judgement, Rosh Hashanah, and the day of atonement, Yom Kippur, both next month.

Why are there two tides per day?

The tides are caused by the gravity of the moon, and so you would expect that we would get one tide per day, following the moon around the earth. But no, there are two. The moon and earth are floating in space and orbiting each other, and the moon pulls almost equally on the earth and on the water. But not quite. The water on the side of the earth closest to the moon gets a slightly stronger pull than the earth and so tries to move ahead, towards the moon, causing one of the tides. The water on the side of the earth farthest from the moon gets a slightly weaker pull and tries to lag behind, causing the other. So there are two bulges in the water, giving two high tides per day. The small differences in pull are the result of gravity weakening as the distance from the moon increases.

A

THE SKY

At night

1st–2nd Close approach of the moon, Jupiter and Saturn, visible from 20.00 in the southeast until setting in the southwest at 03.00. They reach maximum altitude of 17 degrees at 00.00.

8th–9th Close approach of the moon and Mars, visible from 23.00 in the east until lost in the dawn at 05.00, 40 degrees above the southern horizon.

12th–13th The Perseids meteor shower, created when the earth passes through the orbit of Comet Swift-Tuttle and our atmosphere burns up its debris and dust. Best views from about 00.00 to 04.00 on the 13th. The radiant (see page 16) will be at an altitude of about 40 degrees in the northeast.

15th Close approach of the moon and Venus, visible in the northeast sky from about 02.00 until lost in the dawn at an altitude of 35 degrees at 05.30.

28th Close approach of the moon, Jupiter and Saturn, visible in the dusk from 20.00 in the southeast until setting in the southwest at midnight. Maximum altitude of 16 degrees at 22.00.

By day

The sun reaches an altitude of 50 degrees in the London sky and 46 degrees in the Glasgow sky at solar midday (13.00 BST/IST) on 21st.

Day length decreases by 1h 51m in Lowestoft, Suffolk, and by 1h 49m in Dunquin, Republic of Ireland.

Earliest sunrise: 1st August, Lowestoft 05.13, Dunquin 06.03.

Latest sunset: 1st August, Lowestoft 20.44, Dunquin 21.31.

Sunrise and set

	Lowestoft		Dunquin	
	Rise	Set	Rise	Set
1st	05.13	20.44	06.03	21.31
2nd	05.15	20.42	06.05	21.29
3rd	05.16	20.40	06.06	21.28
4th	05.18	20.38	06.08	21.26
5th	05.19	20.36	06.10	21.24
6th	05.21	20.35	06.11	21.22
7th	05.23	20.33	06.13	21.20
8th	05.24	20.31	06.14	21.18
9th	05.26	20.29	06.16	21.16
10th	05.27	20.27	06.18	21.15
11th	05.29	20.25	06.19	21.13
12th	05.31	20.23	06.21	21.11
13th	05.32	20.21	06.22	21.09
14th	05.34	20.19	06.24	21.07
15th	05.36	20.17	06.26	21.05
16th	05.37	20.15	06.27	21.03
17th	05.39	20.13	06.29	21.01
18th	05.41	20.11	06.31	20.58
19th	05.42	20.08	06.32	20.56
20th	05.44	20.06	06.34	20.54
21st	05.46	20.04	06.35	20.52
22nd	05.47	20.02	06.37	20.50
23rd	05.49	20.00	06.39	20.48
24th	05.51	19.58	06.40	20.46
25th	05.52	19.55	06.42	20.43
26th	05.54	19.53	06.44	20.41
27th	05.56	19.51	06.45	20.39
28th	05.57	19.49	06.47	20.37
29th	05.59	19.46	06.49	20.34
30th	06.01	19.44	06.50	20.32
31st	06.02	19.42	06.52	20.30

A

THE SEA

Average sea temperature

Ayr:	14.3°C
Sunderland:	15.6°C
Dingle:	15.7°C
Dublin:	14.9°C
Aberystwyth:	15.8°C
Lowestoft:	17.2°C
Poole:	16.6°C
Newquay:	17.1°C

Spring and neap tides

The spring tides are the most extreme tides of the month, with the highest rises and falls, and the neap tides are the least extreme, with the smallest. Exact timings vary around the coast, but expect them around the following dates:

Spring tides: 5th–6th and 20th–21st

Neap tides: 13th–14th and 27th–28th

In the tide timetable opposite, spring tides are shown with an asterisk.

August tide timetable for Dover

For guidance on how to convert this for your local area, see page 8.

	High water		Low water	
	Morning	Afternoon	Morning	Afternoon
1st	09.19	21.50	03.53	16.26
2nd	10.12	22.42	05.07	17.31
3rd	10.56	23.24	06.03	18.23
4th	11.35	–	06.50	19.09
5th*	00.01	12.14	07.29	19.47
6th*	00.37	12.51	08.02	20.21
7th	01.11	13.26	08.30	20.48
8th	01.45	13.59	08.52	21.12
9th	02.17	14.28	09.15	21.38
10th	02.47	14.58	09.45	22.10
11th	03.20	15.35	10.21	22.50
12th	04.09	16.31	11.07	23.45
13th	05.35	17.56	–	12.13
14th	06.53	19.12	01.09	13.47
15th	07.56	20.14	02.28	15.00
16th	08.50	21.08	03.32	15.59
17th	09.37	21.55	04.28	16.53
18th	10.21	22.40	05.20	17.53
19th	11.03	23.22	06.10	18.33
20th*	11.44	–	06.59	19.22
21st*	00.03	12.26	07.43	20.06
22nd	00.45	13.09	08.23	20.48
23rd	01.28	13.53	09.01	21.27
24th	02.12	14.40	09.39	22.07
25th	03.03	15.32	10.21	22.52
26th	04.02	16.33	11.10	23.48
27th	05.14	17.47	–	12.15
28th	06.40	19.21	00.59	13.35
29th	08.05	20.50	02.20	15.01
30th	09.13	21.51	03.35	16.27
31st	10.02	22.36	05.04	17.26

A

NATURE

The hedgerow in August

In the fields alongside the hedgerows, the harvest begins, great clouds of wheat dust being churned into the air by the combine harvesters. The hedgerow's harvest has begun, too, and the hedgerow is full of berries starting to turn full colour – elderberries, brambles, rowan fruits and haws are beginning their ripening. The birds and the little mammals will soon start to eat them and then spread their seed far and wide, so ensuring the next generation of elders and brambles is sown. There are still flowers around, though not so many as in early summer, and they are visited by bumblebees and honeybees, and by red admiral, speckled wood and comma butterflies.

During this warm weather, badgers take some time to dig and extend their setts in preparation for the cooler months, when they will spend more of their time underground. Long-tailed fieldmice are also thinking ahead, building up their larders ready for winter, in a series of tunnels under the hedgerow. They mark the entrances to the tunnels with little piles of stones (which are clearly important as they will repeatedly replace them if they are moved).

In hot weather, crickets in grassy verges will start to stridulate, or chirrup. They are attracting mates and will lay their eggs under tufts of grass to overwinter, hatching next April. In heat the slugs that live in the cool, damp base of the hedgerow will go underground, while a snail will plug up the opening in its shell to retain moisture. Hazel boletes, one of the earliest of the year's hedgerow fungi, may be spotted around the roots of hazels.

MOTHS

puss moth

swallow-tailed moth

poplar hawk moth

A

cinnabar moth

scarlet tiger moth

CHARM OF THE MONTH

White heather

In August the ling heather is coming into full bloom across Scotland's moorlands and glens, turning them beautiful shades of purple. Among this purple sea you might find a rare patch of white heather, which is considered a lucky charm and historically sold at fairs and tucked into bride's bouquets. There are various stories as to why it is lucky, but the root of it might be its rarity – it is thought to be a sport (spontaneous mutation) of purple heather. It was adopted by the clan called Clanranald whose members wore it into battle and won a miraculous victory, and by Clan Macpherson because of the story that a member of the clan fell asleep on a patch after the Battle of Culloden and was missed by an English search party. There seems a good chance that Queen Victoria, with her love of all things Scottish, took the germ of a story and turned it into a full-blown craze, as the earliest confirmed mention of the superstition is found in her hugely popular book *Leaves from the Journal of Our Life in the Highlands from 1848 to 1861*. Nevertheless, it has since been conferring luck on brides and on anyone who manages to track down an elusive sprig.

THE FLOWER GARDEN

August's flower garden picking prompts
Purple or pink dahlias, heads of elderberries from the
hedgerow, and grass or wheat seed heads; a bunch of gladioli,
in a tall vase; honesty seed heads, dill flowers and heleniums.

Jobs in the flower garden

- Sow hardy annuals such as cornflower, calendula,
  Ammi majus, love-in-a-mist, corn poppy and larkspur
  towards the end of the month. This will give them time
  to germinate and grow a little before the winter cold
  stops them. They then have the winter to develop their
  root systems and will be ready to grow in leaps and
  bounds next spring. You will get far earlier flowers
  by starting now.
- Take cuttings of pelargoniums to overwinter in a
  greenhouse or indoors. The bottom of each cutting should
  be just under a leaf node (bump in the stem), and the top
  just above one. Remove any flower buds, push the bottom
  into a little pot of compost and keep on your windowsill.
- Give wisteria a bit of a haircut. It doesn't have to be too
  exact at this time of the year – just a general shearing
  back to prevent it from getting out of hand and to
  encourage it to concentrate its energies on forming flower
  buds rather than more green growth. You can also do a
  more precise prune in winter, cutting back to two or three
  buds' worth of growth, but if the summer pruning is all
  you can manage, then it will do.

A

THE KITCHEN GARDEN

This is your very last chance to sow root crops for winter. Choose autumn varieties of carrot such as 'Autumn King 2' and 'Red Samurai', and make a final sowing of beetroot at the same time. Plant out cauliflowers for winter and spring, covering them with a brassica cage. Switch to sowing hardy winter lettuce this month, such as 'Merveille de Quatre Saisons' and 'Brighton'. Watch your tomatoes for blight, which can be carried in on rain in late summer. Tomatoes can also suffer from blossom end rot at this time of year, caused by irregular watering. Keep up with your watering and feeding and you shouldn't have a problem. At this time of year you can sometimes get hold of seed potatoes that have been held in storage and will give you new potatoes at Christmas. Plant them into the bottom of big containers that can be wrapped or moved into a greenhouse if frost threatens them close to Christmas. Make a sowing of herbs in pots that can be moved onto the kitchen windowsill to see you into autumn.

Sowing and planting crops

Fruit/veg	Sow under cover	Sow direct	Plant
Spring cabbages	✓	✓	
Kohlrabi		✓	
Kale			✓
Winter cauliflowers			✓
Spring cauliflowers			✓
Lettuces	✓	✓	
Salad leaves	✓	✓	
Winter purslane	✓	✓	
Chicory and radicchio	✓		
Spring onions	✓	✓	
Oriental leaves	✓	✓	✓
Spinach and Swiss chard		✓	
Basil	✓		
Parsley	✓	✓	

Fruit/veg	Sow under cover	Sow direct	Plant
Chervil	✓	✓	
Carrots		✓	
Beetroot		✓	
Turnips		✓	
Winter radishes		✓	
Overwintering onions			✓
Strawberries			✓
Christmas potatoes			✓

A

THE KITCHEN

Sauce of the month – *sugo di pomodoro crudo* (raw tomato sauce)

This sauce only works with the very best ingredients, so make it now with your ripest tomatoes, running with juice and warmed by the sun. Skin 600g tomatoes by cutting a cross in their base, putting them in a bowl and covering them with just-boiled water. Pour the water off after a few minutes, and the skins should come away easily. Chop the tomatoes to bite-size and put them into a large bowl, squeezing them slightly to start releasing the juices. Add a handful of torn basil leaves, plus two lightly bashed garlic cloves, 100ml extra virgin olive oil, two or three really good pinches of sea salt flakes and a few grinds of pepper. Mix and let sit at room temperature for two to three hours. Toss with hot spaghetti, top with grated Pecorino Romano, and serve.

In season

Vegetables: tomatoes, sweet peppers, chilli peppers, aubergines, sweetcorn, courgettes, summer squash, carrots, kohlrabi, Florence fennel, French and runner beans, peas, mangetout, sugar snap peas, spring onions, potatoes, beetroot, turnips, lettuces, chicory, spinach, globe artichokes, cucumbers, radishes, red and summer cabbages, calabrese, summer and autumn cauliflowers, garlic, shallots
Herbs: marjoram, thyme, dill, basil, mint, oregano
Fruits and nuts: crab apples, elderberries, sea buckthorn, cobnuts, figs, melons, plums, raspberries, blackcurrants, cherries, redcurrants, tayberries, apricots, peaches, blueberries, blackberries, strawberries, early ripening apples and pears
Fish: plaice, mackerel, sardines, megrim sole, squid, crab, lobster, scallops

RECIPES

Fennel and cobnut gratin

Vegetables are coming thick and fast from the vegetable plot now, and this is one of the ways you can make use of them. It uses fennel, but baby leeks and young root crops also work well in a gratin, as do brassicas such as Brussels sprouts and purple sprouting broccoli later in the year.

Serves 4 as a side dish, serves 2 as a main
Ingredients
3 large fennel bulbs, cut into 8 pieces down their middles, keeping a piece of core intact
50g butter, melted
75g cobnuts or hazelnuts, roughly chopped
75g Parmesan cheese, grated
Salt and pepper

Method
Preheat your oven to 200°C, Gas Mark 6. Put the fennel pieces and the melted butter on a large baking tray, and toss the fennel pieces in the butter so that they are completely covered. Roast for around 40 minutes, turning once, until the pieces are tender when tested with the point of a knife and the edges are starting to caramelise. Transfer all to a smaller baking dish. Mix together the nuts, Parmesan, salt and pepper and sprinkle over the top. Bake for 30–40 minutes until browned on top.

A

A SONG FOR AUGUST'S FULL MOON

'Moon Shine Tonight'
Traditional, arr. Richard Barnard

A Jamaican folk song from a time when there was no electricity to illuminate night-time gatherings, and it made sense to time parties for the full moon, and then dance and sing in its light.

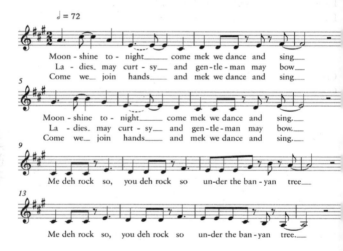

Moon shine tonight come mek we dance and sing.
Moon shine tonight come mek we dance and sing.

>   *Mi deh rock so*
>   *You de rock so*
>   *Under the banyan tree.*
>   *Mi deh rock so*
>   *You deh rock so*
>   *Under the banyan tree.*

Ladies may curtsy and gentleman may bow.
Ladies may curtsy and gentleman may bow.

>   *Chorus*

Come we join hands and mek we dance and sing.
Come we join hands and mek we dance and sing.

A

September

THE MOON

Names for September's full moon – Wine Moon, Song Moon

Strictly speaking, the name Harvest Moon should be applied
to the full moon that falls closest to the autumnal equinox.
Most of the time that falls in September, but this year it is
the first of October's two full moons, falling on 1st October.
But the idea of the harvest moon is useful here to conjure up
the atmosphere of past Septembers, as are the names Wine
Moon and Song Moon. They suggest a time of hard work
and hard play. Harvest time would have meant a great gathering
of people pulled from neighbouring villages to do the most
important farm job of the year in a short time, and those
people needed to be fed, wined and entertained. The light
of the full moon would have extended harvesting hours, as
well as carousing ones.

Moon phases

Full moon – *2nd September, 05.22*

3rd quarter – *10th September, 09.26*

New moon – *17th September, 11.00*

1st quarter – *24th September, 01.55*

Moonrise and set

	Lowestoft		*Dunquin*		
	Rise	Set	Rise	Set	
1st	19.58	04.40	20.46	05.32	
2nd	20.15	05.52	21.04	06.44	full moon
3rd	20.31	07.03	21.20	07.54	
4th	20.45	08.12	21.34	09.03	
5th	20.59	09.20	21.49	10.11	
6th	21.14	10.28	22.04	11.18	
7th	21.31	11.36	22.22	12.26	
8th	21.52	12.45	22.43	13.35	
9th	22.18	13.54	23.09	14.44	
10th	22.52	15.02	23.44	15.51	3rd quarter
11th	23.37	16.05	–	16.54	
12th	–	17.01	00.30	17.49	
13th	00.35	17.46	01.28	18.35	
14th	01.46	18.22	02.39	19.11	
15th	03.06	18.51	04.00	19.39	
16th	04.32	19.14	05.25	20.03	
17th	06.01	19.34	06.53	20.23	new moon
18th	07.29	19.53	08.21	20.43	
19th	08.58	20.12	09.50	21.03	
20th	10.27	20.34	11.18	21.24	
21st	11.54	20.59	12.45	21.51	
22nd	13.18	21.31	14.08	22.23	
23rd	14.35	22.13	15.25	23.05	
24th	15.41	23.05	16.30	23.58	1st quarter
25th	16.33	–	17.21	–	
26th	17.12	00.08	18.00	01.01	
27th	17.42	01.17	18.30	02.10	
28th	18.04	02.29	18.53	03.21	
29th	18.23	03.41	19.11	04.33	
30th	18.38	04.52	19.27	05.43	

S

Where moonset times are before moonrise times, this is the setting of the previous night's moon.

Gardening by the moon

1st quarter to full moon: 1st–2nd and 24th–30th. Sow crops that develop above ground. Plant seedlings and young plants.

Full moon to 3rd quarter: 2nd–10th. Harvest crops for immediate eating. Harvest fruit.

3rd quarter to new moon: 10th–17th. Prune. Harvest for storage. Fertilise and mulch the soil.

New moon to 1st quarter: 17th–24th. Sow crops that develop below ground. Dig the soil.

September moon dates

2nd and 17th – full moon and new moon: best fishing days. Some fishermen believe that fish bite best in the 45 minutes either side of moonrise and set on the full and new moons. So that would be 90 minutes from 05.07 and 19.30 on the 2nd, and from 05.16 and 18.49 on the 17th (Lowestoft times).

17th – new moon in Virgo. This month's new moon is in routine-focused Virgo, and astrologers believe this is a time for making fresh starts around health and organisation. You will see the fruits of this labour around the Virgo full moon on 27th February 2021.

18th (predicted) – day after the sighting of the new crescent moon: the start of Islamic month of Safar. The word 'Safar' can mean 'empty', referring to houses being empty while the household is out gathering the harvest. It can also mean 'whistling of the wind' or 'yellow', perhaps for the colour of the Autumn leaves. However, like all Islamic months, Safar moves through the Gregorian calendar over time, so will not always fall in September.

19th – day after the calculated first sighting of the new crescent moon: the start of Tishrei. The name for the Jewish month of Tishrei comes from the Hebrew word for 'beginning'. This is the start of the Jewish civil year. The first day of Tishrei is Rosh Hashanah, which means 'head of the year'.

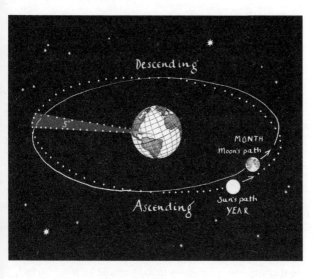

Why aren't there more eclipses?

As you will have seen in February (see page 37), the phases
of the moon are caused by the moon's passage around the
earth over the course of a month, and the sun reflecting off
different portions of it depending on whether the moon is on
the sun's side (new moon), the far side of the earth (full moon)
or somewhere in between. An obvious question then is: if the
moon is between the earth and the sun once a month, and the
earth is between the sun and the moon once a month, why
don't we have two eclipses per month, one lunar and one solar?
The reason is that the moon's path around us and the ecliptic
(the path of the sun through our sky) are just slightly off – by
5 degrees at the most extreme point. The paths cross twice each
month, and these crossing points are called nodes. For a full
lunar or full solar eclipse to occur, a full moon has to coincide
exactly with a node.

THE SKY

At night

5th–6th Close approach of the moon and Mars, visible from 21.30 in the east, until lost in the dawn at 06.30 in the southwest. Their highest point will be an altitude of 45 degrees at 03.30 in the south.

14th Close approach of the moon and Venus, visible in the east from about 03.30 until lost in the dawn at 06.30 at an altitude of 36 degrees.

25th Close approach of the moon, Jupiter and Saturn, visible in the dusk from 19.00 in the southeast until setting in the southwest at 23.30. Maximum altitude of 16 degrees at 20.00.

By day

The autumnal equinox falls on 22nd September at 14.31. The equinox is the moment at which the centre of the sun is directly above the equator, and so day and night are of equal length all around the globe. It occurs twice a year, in March and September.

The sun reaches an altitude of 38 degrees in the London sky and 34 degrees in the Glasgow sky at solar midday (13.00 BST/IST) on the autumnal equinox on 22nd September.

Day length decreases by 1h 57m in Lowestoft, Suffolk, and by 1h 58m in Dunquin, Republic of Ireland.

Earliest sunrise: 1st September, Lowestoft 06.04, Dunquin 06.54.

Latest sunset: 1st September, Lowestoft 19.39, Dunquin 20.28.

Sunrise and set

	Lowestoft		Dunquin	
	Rise	Set	Rise	Set
1st	06.04	19.39	06.54	20.28
2nd	06.06	19.37	06.55	20.25
3rd	06.07	19.35	06.57	20.23
4th	06.09	19.33	06.58	20.21
5th	06.11	19.30	07.00	20.19
6th	06.12	19.28	07.02	20.16
7th	06.14	19.26	07.03	20.14
8th	06.16	19.23	07.05	20.12
9th	06.17	19.21	07.07	20.09
10th	06.19	19.18	07.08	20.07
11th	06.21	19.16	07.10	20.05
12th	06.22	19.14	07.12	20.02
13th	06.24	19.11	07.13	20.00
14th	06.26	19.09	07.15	19.58
15th	06.27	19.07	07.16	19.55
16th	06.29	19.04	07.18	19.53
17th	06.31	19.02	07.20	19.51
18th	06.32	19.00	07.21	19.48
19th	06.34	18.57	07.23	19.46
20th	06.36	18.55	07.25	19.43
21st	06.37	18.52	07.26	19.41
22nd	06.39	18.50	07.28	19.39
23rd	06.41	18.48	07.30	19.36
24th	06.42	18.45	07.31	19.34
25th	06.44	18.43	07.33	19.32
26th	06.46	18.41	07.35	19.29
27th	06.47	18.38	07.36	19.27
28th	06.49	18.36	07.38	19.25
29th	06.51	18.33	07.40	19.22
30th	06.53	18.31	07.41	19.20

S

THE SEA

Average sea temperature

Ayr:	14.2°C
Sunderland:	14.7°C
Dingle:	15.1°C
Dublin:	14.8°C
Aberystwyth:	15.8°C
Lowestoft:	15.6°C
Poole:	17.0°C
Newquay:	16.3°C

Spring and neap tides

The spring tides are the most extreme tides of the month, with the highest rises and falls, and the neap tides are the least extreme, with the smallest. Exact timings vary around the coast, but expect them around the following dates:

Spring tides: 3rd–4th and 29th–2oth

Neap tides: 11th–12th and 25th–26th

In the tide timetable opposite, spring tides are shown with an asterisk.

September tide timetable for Dover

For guidance on how to convert this for your local area, see page 8.

| | High water | | Low water | |
	Morning	Afternoon	Morning	Afternoon
1st	10.42	23.12	05.54	18.14
2nd	11.18	23.44	06.35	18.53
3rd*	11.53	–	07.08	19.26
4th*	00.14	12.27	07.35	19.52
5th	00.44	12.58	07.56	20.13
6th	01.12	13.23	08.15	20.34
7th	01.34	13.42	08.40	21.00
8th	01.53	14.06	09.10	21.30
9th	02.20	14.40	09.44	22.06
10th	02.59	15.26	10.23	22.51
11th	03.55	16.47	11.17	–
12th	06.17	18.46	00.00	12.55
13th	07.29	19.54	01.55	14.30
14th	08.27	20.49	03.07	15.34
15th	09.16	21.37	04.06	16.30
16th	10.00	22.21	05.00	17.23
17th	10.42	23.02	05.51	18.14
18th	11.23	23.42	06.38	19.03
19th*	–	12.04	07.22	19.46
20th*	00.22	12.46	08.01	20.26
21st	01.04	13.29	08.38	21.03
22nd	01.49	14.15	09.16	21.42
23rd	02.38	15.08	09.57	22.25
24th	03.37	16.10	10.45	23.21
25th	04.48	17.26	11.52	–
26th	06.13	19.14	00.38	13.20
27th	07.49	20.46	02.10	15.00
28th	08.57	21.39	03.46	16.17
29th	09.42	22.18	04.46	17.09
30th	10.20	22.50	05.30	17.52

S

NATURE

The hedgerow in September

This is the second great harvest month in the hedgerow year. The hedgerow is dripping with abundant fruits turning fat and shiny, and the hazelnuts are maturing and dropping to the ground. Even the honeysuckle has switched from flowering to berrying. The bramble harvest is in its final throes, and the leaves start to take on shades of autumn, as do the leaves on the rowan trees. Crab apples start to fall. The small mammals – wood mouse, bank vole, hedgehog, common shrew and hazel dormouse – scurry about laying food aside for the winter or feeding themselves up for a long sleep. Sometimes hedgehogs produce a second set of hoglets in September, but these babies will struggle to fatten up in time for winter hibernation and may not make it through the winter, snaffled hazelnuts or no. Fiery milkcap mushrooms may appear near the roots of hazels.

There are increasingly fewer butterflies around, though you may see small tortoiseshells and red admirals. Some caterpillars start to form chrysalises in which to overwinter around now, while most others prepare to overwinter as caterpillars. Wasps, which have been feeding on aphids all summer and being rewarded by their queen with sweet treats, are kicked out of their nests around now, and so they hungrily seek out sweetness in hedgerow berries and fallen crab apples. On warm autumn mornings, tiny money spiders climb to the top of the hedgerow, spin a line and let it catch the gentle breeze, then lift off to fresh territories.

SMALL MAMMALS

hazel dormouse

harvest mouse

bank vole

THE FLOWER GARDEN

September's flower garden picking prompts

A big arrangement of fennel seed heads and sunflowers; a couple of fruiting stems of bramble, some crocosmia and a few poppy seed heads; a single dahlia flower, floating on the surface of a small bowl of water.

Jobs in the flower garden

- Plant pots of miniature irises now to give yourself late-winter floral treats. Plant a handful of bulbs of *Iris reticulata* 'Harmony', *I. histrioides* or *I. danfordiae* in each of a few small pots, and keep them indoors somewhere cool and bright. They will flower in February and you can enjoy them on your kitchen windowsill.
- Sow an annual meadow. It doesn't need to be acres. If you have a bare patch and would like to try to fill it with annual meadow flowers next year, this is the moment. Sow seed across it and then leave it to germinate. You shouldn't need to interfere with it, but do keep an eye out for weeds and remove them.
- The cracks in your path, patio or steps will get filled one way or another – it will be by weeds if you leave them be, so sow seeds in them now instead. Push compost into cracks and sow erigeron, thyme or marjoram now – or buy small plants of non-flowering chamomile 'Treneague', stuff them into the cracks and keep them well watered.

THE KITCHEN GARDEN

This is mainly a month of harvesting. Sow green manures in areas that you have cleared, to protect the soil over winter and improve the soil's structure. Keep feeding tomato plants to encourage ripening, but towards the end of the month you may have to admit that any green ones are going to stay green, and turn to chutney making. Place tiles or pieces of wood under winter squash and pumpkins to prevent them from rotting where they touch the soil. There are still a few leafy vegetables – winter purslane, Oriental leaves, winter lettuces – that you can sow this month for leaves over winter, but it is a good idea to sow them in a greenhouse or polytunnel, or to cover them with cloches, to prevent the leaves from getting battered and tough over winter. Plant some strawberries, peaches or nectarines this month before the weather gets too cold.

Sowing and planting crops

Fruit/veg	Sow under cover	Sow direct	Plant
Spring cabbages			✓
Kale			✓
Lettuces	✓	✓	✓
Rocket	✓	✓	✓
Radishes	✓	✓	
Salad leaves	✓	✓	✓
Winter purslane	✓	✓	
Spring onions	✓	✓	
Oriental leaves	✓	✓	✓
Spinach	✓	✓	✓
Chervil	✓	✓	✓
Coriander	✓	✓	✓
Parsley	✓	✓	✓
Strawberries			✓
Overwintering onions			✓
Peaches and nectarines			✓

S

THE KITCHEN

Sauce of the month – pontack sauce

This is an old English recipe, a beautiful deep wine-purple pouring sauce for eating with the game that comes into season this month, and which makes good use of the abundant elderberries in the hedgerow. Start by stripping 650g elderberries from their stalks, using a fork to pop them off; take your time, as the stalks are toxic. Put them into a large pan with 500ml red wine vinegar, five finely chopped shallots, four cloves, four allspice berries, half a finely grated nutmeg, 2.5cm piece of peeled root ginger, and two teaspoons black peppercorns. Bring to the boil and then simmer for 40–60 minutes. Strain through a fine sieve, pushing down on the berries to release the juice. Return to a clean pan with 200g caster sugar and heat gently to dissolve the sugar, then boil for ten minutes to thicken the sauce. Serve immediately, or pour into sterilised bottles or jars and store for up to a year.

In season

Vegetables: tomatoes, aubergines, chillies, sweet peppers, Florence fennel, courgettes, spinach, sweet potatoes, runner beans, French beans, peas, cucumbers, globe artichokes, sweetcorn, beetroot, calabrese, red cabbage, kohlrabi, cauliflowers, carrots, salad leaves, Swiss chard, Oriental leaves, onions, maincrop potatoes, leeks, kale, turnips, swede, leeks, winter squash, celeriac
Herbs: basil, mint, dill, oregano, thyme, marjoram
Fruit: apples, pears, grapes, figs, melons, plums, apricots, peaches, blackberries, blueberries, raspberries
Meat: grouse, partridge, duck, goose, guinea fowl
Fish: crab, scallops, lobster, hake, megrim sole, sardines, mackerel

RECIPES

Dukkah-fried green tomatoes

By now we are reaching the point at which we have to admit
that our tomatoes are not going to do a whole lot more
ripening, but fear not, because green tomatoes are delicious.
More like vegetables and less sweet than ripened tomatoes, they
really lend themselves to cooking. Fried green tomatoes are
a once-a-year treat, so don't miss them. Dukkah is a Middle
Eastern condiment made from hazelnuts, dried chilli, sesame
seeds, coriander seeds, cumin seeds and salt, which you can
pick up in any supermarket, and it works well to flavour the
crunchy coating.

Serves 4 as a snack or a starter
Ingredients
70g panko breadcrumbs
3 tablespoons dukkah
4 tablespoons plain flour
2 eggs, lightly beaten
Sunflower or vegetable oil for frying
450g green tomatoes (larger ones are better), cut into 2cm-thick slices
Flaky sea salt

S

Method
Set out three plates next to your cooker and tip the panko
breadcrumbs and dukkah into one; mix. Put the flour on a
second plate and the beaten egg on the third. Heat 1cm oil in a
frying pan. Take one tomato slice at a time and dust it all over
with the flour. Now dunk both sides into the egg and then into
the breadcrumb mixture. Lower it carefully into the hot oil, and
continue with more slices until there are a few pieces in the pan.

Fry them gently until they are brown on each side, then transfer them to a heatproof plate lined with kitchen paper. Keep them warm in a low oven while you prepare and cook the remainder in the same way. When they are all cooked, sprinkle them with sea salt flakes and serve them with Tahini and Yoghurt Sauce (see page 218). Be careful when eating them, as the insides are extremely hot just after cooking.

Suffolk Fourses Cakes

There are understandable cries of anguish when hot cross buns appear in shops at times well away from Easter – but the briefest glance at British culinary history will reveal that there is a yeasted, spiced, fruited and sweetened bread for almost any moment in the year. This is one (no doubt of several) for taking out into the fields and eating during harvest time. The perfect excuse to eat fare resembling hot cross buns in September. The name comes from the traditional practice at harvest time of taking midday and mid-afternoon refreshments to the workers in the fields, so 'fourses' has a similar derivation to the more familiar 'elevenses'. This is a lardy bread and so is traditionally made with lard, but you can substitute butter if you prefer. It is a slightly tweaked version of a recipe from the wonderful *Cattern Cakes and Lace* by Julia Jones and Barbara Deer.

Makes 2 loaves
Ingredients
675g strong white flour, plus extra for dusting
1½ teaspoons easy-blend instant dried yeast
½ teaspoon salt
2 teaspoons mixed ground spice

| 2 teaspoons sugar |
| 175g softened lard or butter |
| 450ml warm water |
| 175g currants |

Method

Sift the flour, yeast, salt, spice and sugar into a large bowl, then add the lard or butter and rub it in until it resembles breadcrumbs. Stir in the water and mix until it becomes a dough, then turn out onto a floured surface and knead for 10 minutes. Place it in a clean large bowl, and leave it somewhere warm to rise for 1–2 hours, until doubled in size. Turn it out and knead in the currants, then divide it into two pieces. Shape them into two loaves and put each in a 450g loaf tin. Leave to double in size again.

Preheat the oven to 200°C, Gas Mark 6, and when the loaves have risen enough, bake them for 45 minutes. Leave to cool in the tin for 10 minutes, then turn out onto a wire rack and allow to cool completely before taking into the fields with a bread knife and a pack of cold butter.

S

CHARM OF THE MONTH

Corn dollies

The corn spirit lives in the crop, and at harvest time it is made homeless, which can't be good. The idea of the 'spirit of the corn' – corn being a generic name for grain crops such as wheat and barley – was prevalent in pre-Christian, pagan communities throughout Europe. It must have at its heart the vast importance of this crop to the communities that farmed it. Sometimes the corn spirit is male – see the well-known folk song 'John Barleycorn' for a manly personification – but the idea of the 'corn mother' and 'corn maiden' was strong, too. The harvest would have been carried out by gangs of men, women and children, and the cutting of the final sheaf of corn took on a great significance, representing the end of a period of extremely hard work, the beginning of the harvest feast, and the housing of the spirit of the corn itself. This final sheaf was held up and proclaimed, then taken away and woven or plaited into a dolly that became the centrepiece of the end-of-harvest celebrations. After this, the dolly would be safely housed to keep the spirit of the corn happy over the winter, and in the spring it was ploughed into the earth with the new crop's seeds.

A SONG FOR SEPTEMBER'S FULL MOON

'Autumn Comes, the Summer is Past' ('Under the Harvest Moon')
Traditional, arr. Richard Barnard

Normally the harvest moon falls in September, but this year's falls on 1st October. Nevertheless, September's full moon still falls during the harvest and will be just as big and yellow as the official harvest moon in October. This 16th-century English song, with its slightly mournful air, captures the feeling of summer slipping away under its golden light.

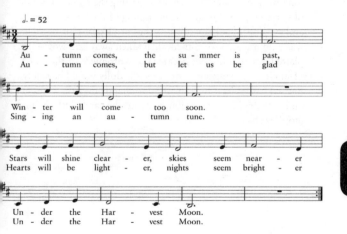

Au – tumn comes, the su – mmer is past,
Au – tumn comes, but let us be glad

Win – ter will come too soon.
Sing – ing an au – tumn tune.

Stars will shine clear – er, skies seem near – er
Hearts will be light – er, nights seem bright – er

Un – der the Har – vest Moon.
Un – der the Har – vest Moon.

S

October

3 First day of Tabernacles – Sukkot (Jewish)

17 17th–25th: Navaratri – autumn festival (Hindu)

21 Apple Day

22 Stow Horse Fair – autumn gypsy/Roma/traveller gathering

25 British Summer Time and Irish Standard Time end. Clocks go back one hour at 02.00

26 October bank holiday, Republic of Ireland

29 Prophet Muhammad's birthday (Muslim) – celebrations begin at sundown on 28th

31 Hallowe'en

THE MOON

Names for October's two Full Moons – Harvest Moon and Hunter's Moon or Blood Moon

October this year contains two full moons, one at the very beginning and one at the end. You will sometimes see the second moon within a month referred to as a 'blue moon', but this is fairly modern nomenclature, and, in fact, October's two full moons have distinct and very old names. The first full moon of the month, being the closest to the autumnal equinox, is called the Harvest Moon, and suggests precious working hours extended by its helpful silvery light, so that the harvest can be successfully brought in. The second – the Hunter's Moon or Blood Moon – is also named in praise of its helpful rays, suggesting the creation of perfect hunting and slaughtering conditions. Deer and livestock have fattened up over the summer, making October the time to hunt, slaughter and stock up on meat for winter. The combination of the leaves starting to fall from the trees and the bright light of a full moon would have made for a particularly excellent hunting night.

Moon phases

Full moon – *1st October, 21.05*

3rd quarter – *10th October, 00.40*

New moon – *16th October, 19.31*

1st quarter – *23rd October, 13.23*

Full moon – *31st October, 14.49*

Moonrise and set

	Lowestoft		*Dunquin*		
	Rise	Set	Rise	Set	
1st	18.52	06.01	19.42	06.52	full moon
2nd	19.06	07.09	19.56	08.00	
3rd	19.20	08.17	20.10	09.08	
4th	19.36	09.26	20.27	10.16	
5th	19.55	10.35	20.46	11.25	
6th	20.18	11.44	21.10	12.34	
7th	20.49	12.52	21.40	13.41	
8th	21.28	13.56	22.21	14.45	
9th	22.20	14.54	23.13	15.42	
10th	23.24	15.42	–	16.30	3rd quarter
11th	–	16.21	00.17	17.09	
12th	00.38	16.51	01.31	17.39	
13th	02.00	17.15	02.53	18.04	
14th	03.26	17.36	04.18	18.25	
15th	04.54	17.55	05.46	18.44	
16th	06.23	18.14	07.15	19.03	new moon
17th	07.54	18.34	08.45	19.24	
18th	09.25	18.57	10.16	19.48	
19th	10.54	19.27	11.45	20.19	
20th	12.19	20.05	13.08	20.58	
21st	13.32	20.55	14.21	21.48	
22nd	14.31	21.56	15.19	22.49	
23rd	15.15	23.05	16.03	23.58	1st quarter
24th	15.48	–	16.36	–	
25th	15.12	00.17	16.00	01.10	
26th	15.31	00.30	16.19	01.22	
27th	15.47	01.41	16.36	02.33	
28th	16.01	02.51	16.50	03.43	
29th	16.14	03.59	17.04	04.51	
30th	16.28	05.07	17.18	05.58	
31st	16.43	06.16	17.33	07.06	full moon

British Summer Time and Irish Standard Time end on 25th October at 02.00, and this is accounted for above.
Where moonset times are before moonrise times, this is the setting of the previous night's moon.

Gardening by the moon

1st quarter to full moon: 1st and 23rd–31st. Sow crops that develop above ground. Plant seedlings and young plants.

Full moon to 3rd quarter: 1st–10th and 31st. Harvest crops for immediate eating. Harvest fruit.

3rd quarter to new moon: 10th–16th. Prune. Harvest for storage. Fertilise and mulch the soil.

New moon to 1st quarter: 16th–23rd. Sow crops that develop below ground. Dig the soil.

October moon dates

1st, 16th and 31st – full moons and new moon: best fishing days. Some fishermen believe that fish bite best in the 45 minutes either side of moonrise and set on the full and new moons. So that would be 90 minutes from 05.16 and 18.07 on the 1st, from 05.38 and 17.29 on the 16th, and from 05.31 and 15.58 on the 31st (Lowestoft times).

16th – new moon in Libra. This month's new moon is in harmonious Libra – astrologers believe this is a time to think about negotiations and diplomacy. You will see the fruits of this labour during the Libra full moon on 28th March 2021.

18th (predicted) – day after the sighting of the new crescent moon: the start of Rabi' al-Awwal. The Islamic month of Rabi' al-Awwal is the month that Muhammad was born, and so this is a very holy month.

19th – day after the calculated first sighting of the new crescent moon: the start of Cheshvan. The Jewish month of Cheshvan is sometimes known as mar-Cheshvan, or 'bitter Cheshvan', as it contains no festivals and marks the start of colder months.

31st – full moon: Loi Krathong. Buddhist celebration, held at the second full moon this month. Loi Krathong means 'floating basket'. Small baskets are made from *krathong* (leaves), filled with candles, incense, flowers and food, and floated on rivers. Wishes are made, and the baskets are said to take bad luck away with them.

The moon illusion

The Harvest Moon is one of the most remarked-upon full moons of the year, noted for being huge and orange. The colour is related to the harvest: crop harvesting throws lots of dust up into the atmosphere, which scatters green, blue and purple light waves so that we are left looking at the red, orange and yellow, particularly when the moon is low.

The apparent size is down to the 'moon illusion', whereby the moon always looks larger when it is closer to the horizon. In fact, it is always roughly the same size, but landscape features like trees, mountains and buildings appear smaller the farther away they are, and when the moon is close to the horizon we directly compare the visual sizes of distant objects with the visual size of the moon. A distant tree might be completely silhouetted by the moon, making the moon appear huge. We cannot do this when the moon is high in the sky. Added to this is the timing of this particular moon. The full moon always rises just after the sun sets. Through summer this has been pretty late in the evening but, now that we are past the equinox, it is suddenly much earlier. We might be more likely to be out and about and so more likely to spot it actually rising above the horizon, and looking its largest and its most golden.

THE SKY

At night

2nd–3rd Close approach of the moon and Mars, visible from 19.30 in the east, until lost at 06.00 in the west. They will reach an altitude of 44 degrees at 02.30 in the south.

13th–14th Mars is at opposition, which means that it will be at its brightest and largest tonight. Visible from 18.30 in the east, it reaches an altitude of 44 degrees at midnight in the south before setting in the west at 07.00.

14th Close approach of the moon and Venus, visible in the east from about 04.00 and until they are lost in the dawn at 07.00 at an altitude of 30 degrees.

21st–22nd Orionids meteor shower: a medium-intensity shower caused by the burning up of debris when the earth meets the orbit of Halley's Comet again (see page 104). Peaks pre-dawn with up to 20 meteors per hour.

22nd Close approach of the moon, Jupiter and Saturn, visible in the dusk from 18.00 in the south until setting in the southwest at 21.30. Maximum altitude of 14 degrees.

29th–30th Close approach of the moon and Mars, visible from 17.00 in the east, until 04.30 in the west, after reaching an altitude of 44 degrees at 01.30 in the south.

By day

The sun reaches an altitude of 28 degrees in the London sky and 24 degrees in the Glasgow sky at solar midday (13.00 BST/IST) on 21st October.

Day length decreases by 1h 58m in Lowestoft, Suffolk, and by 1h 56m in Dunquin, Republic of Ireland.

Earliest sunrise: 1st October, Lowestoft 06.54, Dunquin 07.43.

Latest sunset: 1st October, Lowestoft 18.29, Dunquin 19.18.

Sunrise and set

	Lowestoft		Dunquin	
	Rise	Set	Rise	Set
1st	06.54	18.29	07.43	19.18
2nd	06.56	18.26	07.45	19.15
3rd	06.58	18.24	07.46	19.13
4th	06.59	18.22	07.48	19.11
5th	07.01	18.19	07.50	19.09
6th	07.03	18.17	07.51	19.06
7th	07.05	18.15	07.53	19.04
8th	07.06	18.13	07.55	19.02
9th	07.08	18.10	07.57	18.59
10th	07.10	18.08	07.58	18.57
11th	07.11	18.06	08.00	18.55
12th	07.13	18.04	08.02	19.53
13th	07.15	18.01	08.03	18.51
14th	07.17	17.59	08.05	18.48
15th	07.19	17.57	08.07	18.46
16th	07.20	17.55	08.09	18.44
17th	07.22	17.52	08.10	18.42
18th	07.24	17.50	08.12	18.40
19th	07.26	17.48	08.14	18.38
20th	07.27	17.46	08.16	18.35
21st	07.29	17.44	08.18	18.33
22nd	07.31	17.42	08.19	18.31
23rd	07.33	17.40	08.21	18.29
24th	07.35	17.38	08.23	18.27
25th	06.37	16.36	07.25	17.25
26th	06.38	16.34	07.26	17.23
27th	06.40	16.32	07.28	17.21
28th	06.42	16.30	07.30	17.19
29th	06.44	16.28	07.32	17.17
30th	06.46	16.26	07.34	17.15
31st	06.48	16.24	07.35	17.14

British Summer Time and Irish Standard Time end on 25th October at 02.00, and this is accounted for above.

O

THE SEA

Average sea temperature

Ayr:	13.4°C
Sunderland:	12.6°C
Dingle:	13.8°C
Dublin:	14.1°C
Aberystwyth:	14.7°C
Lowestoft:	15.6°C
Poole:	16.1°C
Newquay:	14.7°C

Spring and neap tides

The spring tides are the most extreme tides of the month, with the highest rises and falls, and the neap tides are the least extreme, with the smallest. Exact timings vary around the coast, but expect them around the following dates:

Spring tides: 3rd–4th and 18th–19th

Neap tides: 11th–12th and 25th–26th

In the tide timetable opposite, spring tides are shown with an asterisk.

October tide timetable for Dover

For guidance on how to convert this for your local area, see page 8.

	High water		*Low water*	
	Morning	Afternoon	Morning	Afternoon
1st	10.54	23.18	06.07	18.27
2nd	11.27	23.46	06.37	18.54
3rd*	11.58	–	07.00	19.15
4th*	00.13	12.25	07.20	19.36
5th	00.37	12.45	07.43	20.00
6th	00.54	13.03	08.11	20.28
7th	01.15	13.29	08.41	20.58
8th	01.44	14.03	09.14	21.33
9th	02.24	14.48	09.53	22.16
10th	03.17	15.55	10.44	23.16
11th	05.40	18.23	–	12.05
12th	07.00	19.31	01.15	13.57
13th	08.00	20.27	02.39	15.06
14th	08.50	21.15	03.40	16.03
15th	09.35	21.59	04.34	16.57
16th	10.17	22.40	05.24	17.50
17th	10.59	23.19	06.12	18.38
18th*	11.40	–	06.56	19.22
19th*	00.00	12.23	07.37	20.02
20th	00.43	13.07	08.16	20.40
21st	01.28	13.54	08.55	21.20
22nd	02.18	14.47	09.38	22.03
23rd	03.16	15.50	10.27	22.59
24th	04.22	17.03	11.35	–
25th	05.39	18.49	00.17	13.03
26th	07.13	20.19	01.47	14.35
27th	08.23	21.10	03.09	15.49
28th	09.10	21.47	04.07	16.35
29th	09.49	22.18	04.52	17.16
30th	10.24	22.47	05.29	17.49
31st	10.56	23.15	05.59	18.15

O

NATURE

The hedgerow in October

All of the hedgerow leaves are now colouring or falling.
Shades of red, yellow, brown and even tinges of purple
cling on between the late hedgerow harvest of rosehips,
elderberries, sloes and haws. Spiders are at their largest and
most mature, with many of them pregnant, too, and they
are highly visible on webs strung extravagantly across the
hedgerow, as if this is their time. The webs catch the dew from
the night mists that begin about now, and the droplets may
even freeze like beautiful strings of jewels as the first frosts of
the year hit.

The hazel dormouse is busy building a new nest especially
for winter, at ground level and sheltered by dead wood, moss
and leaf litter. Dormice will then go into their long and deep
hibernation until next May. Hedgehogs will also go into
hibernation this month or next, and need to eat as much as
they can to build themselves up ahead of this. Badgers do not
hibernate but are feeding on fallen crab apples, brambles and
acorns to put on fat reserves ahead of winter.

With autumn rains, the mosses on dead branches and at
the base of the hedgerow start to produce and release their
spores – their equivalent of seed – which will be carried
through the air to land and germinate on moist soil and
create new mosses. Rains also encourage mushrooms and
other fungal fruiting bodies to appear: ethereal, pure white
porcelain fungi on dead beech, bracket fungi on spindle and
oak, chicken of the woods, beefsteak fungi and many more.

MUSHROOMS

calocera cornea

shaggy ink cap

fairy bath

wood blewit

bolete

O

THE FLOWER GARDEN

October's flower garden picking prompts

Haws from the hedgerow mixed with chrysanthemums and love-in-a-mist seed heads; a bunch of dried hydrangea seed heads; a twig of coppery beech leaves in a little vase.

Jobs in the flower garden

- Start some amaryllis (also known as hippeastrum) bulbs now and you might just time the flowers to coincide with Christmas. Pot the bulbs up with the top halves sticking out of the soil. Water them – lightly at first – to start them into growth, and keep them on a sunny windowsill, turning the pots round frequently as they grow. There are some really unusual varieties available now with narrow-petalled flowers, such as 'Cybister Rose' and 'Evergreen'.

- Rip out and compost old summer bedding and plant up your hanging baskets and window boxes for winter. There are lots of plants in the garden centres now that will flower on and off through winter, chief among them pretty pansies and violas. Pack them in along with evergreen foliage plants – unlike their summer counterparts, they will not grow much.

- The soil is moist and still warm from summer and this is the moment for planting many herbaceous perennials, including Japanese anemone, astrantia, delphinium, perennial wallflower, angelica, euphorbia, helenium, rudbeckia, aster and hellebore. It is also a good time for lifting, dividing and replanting those you already have, if the clumps are getting big and you would like more plants.

THE KITCHEN GARDEN

Cut pumpkins and winter squash and leave them to cure for a few days in the sun, or in a sunny spot in a greenhouse or indoors if no sunny weather is predicted. They need to be tucked away indoors before the first frosts hit. In milder areas carrots, turnips and swede can be dug up throughout winter as they are needed, but in colder spots it is a good idea to lift them now and store them. Harvest and store your apples and pears and dry out beans for storing. Turn your compost heap.

Sowing and planting crops

Fruit/veg	Sow under cover	Sow direct	Plant
Lettuces	✓	✓	✓
Rocket			✓
Salad leaves	✓	✓	✓
Winter purslane	✓	✓	
Oriental leaves	✓	✓	✓
Chervil			✓
Coriander			✓
Parsley			✓
Overwintering onions			✓
Peaches and nectarines			✓
Raspberries			✓

O

THE KITCHEN

Sauce of the month – tahini and yoghurt sauce for roast vegetables

Autumn is prime vegetable-roasting season: all of the greenhouse vegetables that intensify and sweeten when roasted are still around, and they are joined this month by autumn roots and winter cauliflowers, which make a very earthy but equally good oven tray full, perhaps dusted with cumin as they roast. This sauce is one that can be used in lots of ways all year but is particularly good dolloped alongside these vegetables once they have been slow-roasted and topped with a bit of goat's cheese or feta for their last few minutes in the oven.

In a bowl combine three tablespoons of Greek yoghurt, two tablespoons of light tahini, two tablespoons of extra virgin olive oil and the juice of half a lemon. Mix and loosen with more oil if needed. Season generously with salt and pepper. Spoon into a bowl and top with toasted nuts or seeds or with a sprinkling of sumac, and a little more olive oil.

In season

Vegetables: aubergines, tomatoes, chillies, sweet peppers, peas, calabrese, salsify, scorzonera, Jerusalem artichokes, beetroot, carrots, parsnips, turnips, swede, winter radishes, sweet potatoes, celeriac, winter squash, kale, cauliflowers, autumn cabbages, Brussels sprouts, kohlrabi, Oriental leaves, leeks, spinach

Herbs: chervil, parsley, coriander, sage, rosemary, bay

Fruit: apples, pears, quinces, medlars, grapes, figs, raspberries

Fungi: ceps, chanterelles, puffballs, white truffles

Meat: duck, goose, grouse, guinea fowl, hare, pheasant, rabbit, venison

Fish: oysters, hake, lemon sole, sardines, mackerel

RECIPES

Mash of nine sorts, for your unmarried guests on Hallowe'en

Hallowe'en was once closely associated with love divination, and it was one of the key moments in the year for peering into the future. Apple bobbing, or apple dooking in Scotland, was originally used to divine whom you would marry: the first girl to manage to bite into an apple floating in a tub of water would be the first of the next year to marry, and if she slept with that apple under her pillow that night she would dream of her future husband. Mash – as unlikely as it sounds – was also used for this purpose. The 'mash of nine sorts' is a mash containing exactly nine ingredients, into which was pushed a wedding ring. The person who was served up the portion with the ring would be the next to marry. As long as the whole adds up to nine, you can, of course, substitute other ingredients than those shown here (turnips or celeriac are obvious ones), but this combination works beautifully and is much more than the sum of its many parts. It's the perfect accompaniment to sausages and homemade gravy.

Serves 4
Ingredients
100g butter
2 leeks, washed and sliced
450g potatoes, peeled and chopped into chunks
2 large carrots, peeled and chopped into chunks
half a medium swede (about 225g), peeled and chopped into chunks
1 parsnip, peeled, cored, and chopped into chunks
150ml double cream
Salt and pepper

O

Method
Melt half the butter in a pan and add the leeks. Cover and leave to 'sweat' until they are translucent and silky, at least 20 minutes.

Meanwhile, bring two large pans of salted water to the boil, and put the potatoes into one and the other root vegetables into the other. Boil until they are cooked, about 15–20 minutes, then drain and combine in one large pan with the cream, the leeks, the rest of the butter and some salt and pepper.

Mash with a potato masher, but try to leave plenty of chunky bits so that it is not all blended together and so that you can still see the different ingredients. Serve with sausages and gravy.

CHARM OF THE MONTH

Horseshoes

The tradition of hanging a horseshoe for good luck
is particularly prevalent within the gypsy and Roma
communities, who have one of their major gatherings, the
Stowe Horse Fair in Gloucester, this month. Horseshoe
charms are worn as jewellery by the women of the
communities, and real horseshoes hang above the doors
to wagons and caravans. The tale goes that a Roma man
was riding back to his camp one night when he found
himself being pursued by four demons: bad luck, ill health,
unhappiness and death. He raced ahead of them but bad luck
started to catch up, at which point the man's horse's shoe
flew off, hit bad luck on the head, and killed him. The three
demons retreated to bury their brother and the man returned
for the horseshoe, then hung it up above his wagon door to
show that it had killed bad luck.

Finding one on the roadside is the luckiest way to get
your own. Always hang a horseshoe with the ends pointing
upwards, to hold in the luck. A horseshoe is also useful up
the chimney to prevent witches flying down it.

O

A SONG FOR OCTOBER'S FULL MOON

'The Wild, Wild Berry'
Traditional, arr. Richard Barnard

There are two full moons this month and if you are looking for a song for the first, you will need to dip back into September, where the harvest moon is eulogised. This song is for the hunter's moon, October's second full moon, which is at the end of the month and which is a far darker and more eerie thing. The song goes by many different titles and has varying lyrics, but the gist is always that a young man comes home from hunting in the moonlight beset by terrible pains, having met with his false love, who has poisoned him with deadly nightshade in order to be rid of him.

Young man came from hunting faint and weary,
'Oh, what ails my son, my deary?'
'Oh, mother dear, let my bed be made,
For I feel the gripe of the woody nightshade.'
Lie low, sweet Randall.

Now all you young men that do eat full well,
And you that sups right merry:
'Tis a far better treat to have toads for your meat
Than to eat of the wild, wild berry.

Now this young man, well, he died full soon
By the light of the hunter's moon.
Not by the bolt, nor yet by blade
But the gripe of the woody nightshade.
Lie low, sweet Randall.

Chorus

The lordship's love they hanged her high,
For she had caused her lord to die.
In her hair they entwined a braid
Of the leaves and berries of the woody nightshade.
Lie low, sweet Randall.

Chorus

O

November

- **1** Samhain (pagan/neopagan celebration)
- **1** All Saints' Day (Christian)
- **2** All Souls' Day (Christian)
- **5** Guy Fawkes Night
- **7** Bridgwater Carnival
- **8** Remembrance Sunday
- **11** Armistice Day/Remembrance Day
- **11** Martinmas (Christian, traditional)
- **14** Diwali – festival of lights (Hindu/Sikh/Jain)
- **19** Beaujolais Nouveau Day
- **22** Stir-up Sunday
- **26** Thanksgiving (American)
- **29** First Sunday in Advent (Christian)
- **30** St Andrew's Day – patron saint of Scotland

THE MOON

Names for November's full moon – Darkest Depths Moon, Moon Before Yule, Mourning Moon

As we tip farther away from the sun, the nights lengthen and turn colder, and frosts become increasingly likely. There is every chance that the light from November's full moon will fall upon a gently glittering countryside. In gardens the cells within tender garden plants are frozen stiff, to collapse into mush when the morning thaw comes, and those leaves that haven't yet fallen from the trees take these frosts as their final sign to shed their chlorophyll and let their golds and reds shine through, before falling to the ground. The names Darkest Depths Moon is a nice case of stating the obvious, albeit poetically. We are nearly at the very darkest point in the year, and the nights are long and cold; clearly pointing this out once felt pretty important. Moon Before Yule is even more self-evident, but Mourning Moon is something of a puzzle. Perhaps this was connected to the ancient Celtic festival of Samhain or the Christian All Souls' Day, both of which have at their hearts a commemoration of those who have passed away, or perhaps it is a sad farewell to the growing year.

Moon phases

3rd quarter – *8th November, 13.46*

New moon – *15th November, 05.07*

1st quarter – *22nd November, 04.45*

Full moon – *30th November, 09.30*

Moonrise and set

	Lowestoft		Dunquin		
	Rise	Set	Rise	Set	
1st	17.01	07.25	17.51	08.15	
2nd	17.22	08.35	18.13	09.25	
3rd	17.49	09.44	18.41	10.33	
4th	18.25	10.50	19.18	11.39	
5th	19.12	11.50	20.05	12.39	
6th	20.11	12.41	21.04	13.29	
7th	21.20	13.22	22.13	14.10	
8th	22.37	13.54	23.30	14.42	3rd quarter
9th	23.58	14.19	–	15.07	
10th	–	14.40	00.51	15.29	
11th	01.22	14.58	02.15	15.48	
12th	02.48	15.16	03.40	16.06	
13th	04.16	15.34	05.08	16.25	
14th	05.47	15.56	06.38	16.46	
15th	07.18	16.21	08.09	17.13	new moon
16th	08.48	16.55	09.38	17.47	
17th	10.11	17.40	11.00	18.33	
18th	11.19	18.38	12.08	19.31	
19th	12.12	19.47	13.00	20.40	
20th	12.50	21.01	13.38	21.54	
21st	13.17	22.15	14.06	23.08	
22nd	13.38	23.29	14.27	–	1st quarter
23rd	13.55	–	14.44	00.21	
24th	14.10	00.39	14.59	01.31	
25th	14.23	01.48	15.12	02.40	
26th	14.36	02.57	15.26	03.47	
27th	14.51	04.05	15.41	04.55	
28th	15.07	05.14	15.57	06.04	
29th	15.27	06.24	16.18	07.14	
30th	15.52	07.34	16.43	08.23	full moon

Where moonset times are before moonrise times, this is the setting of the previous night's moon.

Gardening by the moon

Full moon to 3rd quarter: 1st–8th. Harvest crops for immediate eating. Harvest fruit.

3rd quarter to new moon: 8th–15th. Prune. Harvest for storage. Fertilise and mulch the soil.

New moon to 1st quarter: 15th–22nd. Sow crops that develop below ground. Dig the soil.

1st quarter to full moon: 22nd–30th. Sow crops that develop above ground. Plant seedlings and young plants.

November moon dates

14th – new moon: Diwali. The Hindu festival of lights coincides with the darkest time of the month: the new moon. Lamps and candles are lit to celebrate the row of lamps that led exiled Rama and Sita back from the forest.

15th – new moon in Scorpio. This month's new moon is in intense Scorpio, and astrologers believe this is a time for planning around personal empowerment and deep desires. The fruits of this will be seen around the Scorpio full moon on 27th April 2021.

15th and 30th – new moon and full moon: best fishing days. Some fishermen believe that fish bite best in the 45 minutes either side of moonrise and set on the new moon and moons. So that would be 90 minutes from 06.33 and 15.36 on the 15th, and from 06.49 and 15.07 on the 30th (Lowestoft times).

16th (predicted) – day after the sighting of the new crescent moon: the start of Rabi' al-Thani. The Islamic month of Rabi' al-Thani is the fourth month of the Islamic year.

17th – day after the calculated first sighting of the new crescent moon: the start of Kislev. The Jewish month of Kislev is known as the 'month of dreams' and the name comes from either a word related to 'rain' or a word meaning 'hope' or 'positivity'. Either way it signifies hope for rains arriving in autumn. Hannukah, the Jewish festival of lights, starts on the 24th day of Kislev (10th December this year).

Peeks at the dark side of the moon – lunar libration

While it is true that the same side of the moon is always facing us (see page 147), that is not quite the full story. We actually see a little more of it – 59 per cent of it over the course of a year – by peeking around its corners. Some of this happens daily (or nightly): as our position on the earth moves from one side to the other, we can see a little more around each side. Some is monthly: although the moon rotates once for each orbit it makes of the earth, always keeping its face towards us, its orbit is variable, and sometimes our rotation pulls slightly ahead of it, allowing a glance to its 'front', and sometimes it lags behind. Finally, there are seasonal changes. Just like the earth, the moon has seasons and it tips on its axis, and so sometimes we can see sneaky peaks beyond the bottom, and sometimes beyond the top.

N

THE SKY

At night

13th Close approach of the moon and Venus, visible in the southeastern sky from about 05.00 until becoming lost in the dawn at 07.30 at an altitude of 20 degrees.

17th–18th Leonids meteor shower. Occasionally has very spectacular years but generally this is a low- to medium-level shower. Created as we pass through the debris of comet 55P/Tempel-Tuttle. It peaks during the early hours of the 18th.

19th Close approach of the moon, Jupiter and Saturn, visible in the dusk from 16.00 in the south until setting in the southwest at 19.30. Its maximum altitude will be 16 degrees.

25th–26th Close approach of the moon and Mars, visible in the twilight from 16.00 in the east, until 02.30 in the west, having reached an altitude of 41 degrees at 20.30 in the south.

By day

Day length decreases by 1h 29m in Lowestoft, Suffolk, and by 1h 28m in Dunquin, Republic of Ireland.

The sun reaches an altitude of 18 degrees in the London sky and 14 degrees in the Glasgow sky at midday on 21st.

Earliest sunrise: 1st November, Lowestoft 06.49, Dunquin 07.37.

Latest sunset: 1st November, Lowestoft 16.22, Dunquin 17.12.

Sunrise and set

	Lowestoft		Dunquin	
	Rise	Set	Rise	Set
1st	06.49	16.22	07.37	17.12
2nd	06.51	16.20	07.39	17.10
3rd	06.53	16.18	07.41	17.08
4th	06.55	16.17	07.43	17.06
5th	06.57	16.15	07.45	17.05
6th	06.59	16.13	07.46	17.03
7th	07.00	16.11	07.48	17.01
8th	07.02	16.10	07.50	17.00
9th	07.04	16.08	07.52	16.58
10th	07.06	16.06	07.54	16.56
11th	07.08	16.05	07.55	16.55
12th	07.09	16.03	07.57	16.53
13th	07.11	16.02	07.59	16.52
14th	07.13	16.00	08.01	16.50
15th	07.15	15.59	08.02	16.49
16th	07.17	15.58	08.04	16.48
17th	07.18	15.56	08.06	16.46
18th	07.20	15.55	08.08	16.45
19th	07.22	15.54	08.09	16.44
20th	07.24	15.52	08.11	16.43
21st	07.25	15.51	08.13	16.41
22nd	07.27	15.50	08.14	16.40
23rd	07.29	15.49	08.16	16.39
24th	07.30	15.48	08.18	16.38
25th	07.32	15.47	08.19	16.37
26th	07.33	15.46	08.21	16.36
27th	07.35	15.45	08.22	16.36
28th	07.36	15.44	08.24	16.35
29th	07.38	15.44	08.25	16.34
30th	07.39	15.43	08.27	16.33

N

THE SEA

Average sea temperature

Ayr:	12.2°C
Sunderland:	10.7°C
Dingle:	12.5°C
Dublin:	13.1°C
Aberystwyth:	13.2°C
Lowestoft:	13.4°C
Poole:	14.3°C
Newquay:	13.3°C

Spring and neap tides

The spring tides are the most extreme tides of the month, with the highest rises and falls, and the neap tides are the least extreme, with the smallest. Exact timings vary around the coast, but expect them around the following dates:

Spring tides: 1st–2nd and 16th–17th

Neap tides: 9th–10th and 23rd–24th

In the tide timetable opposite, spring tides are shown with an asterisk.

November tide timetable for Dover

For guidance on how to convert this for your local area, see page 8.

	High water		*Low water*	
	Morning	Afternoon	Morning	Afternoon
1st*	11.26	23.42	06.24	18.39
2nd*	11.51	–	06.49	19.05
3rd	00.05	12.13	07.17	19.33
4th	00.26	12.35	07.47	20.03
5th	00.50	13.04	08.19	20.35
6th	01.23	13.41	08.54	21.10
7th	02.05	14.28	09.34	21.54
8th	03.02	15.38	10.25	22.52
9th	04.48	17.52	11.39	–
10th	06.22	19.02	00.27	13.20
11th	07.26	20.00	02.01	14.31
12th	08.20	20.49	03.05	15.31
13th	09.07	21.34	04.01	16.27
14th	09.52	22.17	04.55	17.22
15th	10.36	22.59	05.45	18.13
16th*	11.20	23.42	06.32	19.00
17th*	–	12.04	07.17	19.43
18th	00.26	12.49	07.59	20.23
19th	01.12	13.37	08.42	21.04
20th	02.02	14.30	09.26	21.47
21st	02.56	15.29	10.16	22.39
22nd	03.55	16.34	11.17	23.47
23rd	05.00	17.53	–	12.30
24th	06.16	19.23	01.02	13.44
25th	07.31	20.22	02.12	14.49
26th	08.27	21.05	03.12	15.42
27th	09.11	21.40	04.02	16.26
28th	09.49	22.12	04.44	17.02
29th	10.22	22.43	05.19	17.35
30th	10.53	23.13	05.51	18.07

N

NATURE

The hedgerow in November

As the hedgerow turns increasingly brown and bare, there are still flashes of colour to be found. Chief among these are the rosehips, the shiny postbox red of the dog rose and the dark purple of burnet rose, but the bizarre fuchsia and orange spindle fruits give them a run for their money, looking like an art teacher's earrings. Hawthorn leaves turn shades of purple in the cold and their haws a deep red, while guelder rose leaves turn pinky yellow, all the better to make their remaining red fruits stand out. There are strings of bright red woody nightshade berries against bare stems and browning foliage. The fruits of the wayfaring tree are turning from red to black, and the dusty purple sloes are ripe on their bare stems, at their sweetest now after they have been touched by the first frosts. And above all of this hang the fluffy seed heads of wild clematis – old man's beard – looking like strings of fairy lights if they catch the low winter light. The male fern and the soft shield fern have died down, leaving just the evergreen hart's-tongue fern to plod on through winter. Wood blewits have come into season, and beautiful and weird scarlet elf cup fungi appear on dead and decaying wood, as do shaggy parasol mushrooms. The berries on spikes of lords-and-ladies are turning lipstick red. Amid all this ripening and dying down, one plant bucks the trend: ivy starts flowering about now and is visited by grateful wasps, bees and green lacewings that are after the sustaining sips of nectar.

Down at the base of the hedgerow, mammal activity is minimal as the small animals snuggle in burrows or nests against the cold. Deer make use of the hedgerow for shelter against winds and storms.

SEEDHEADS OF THE HEDGEROW

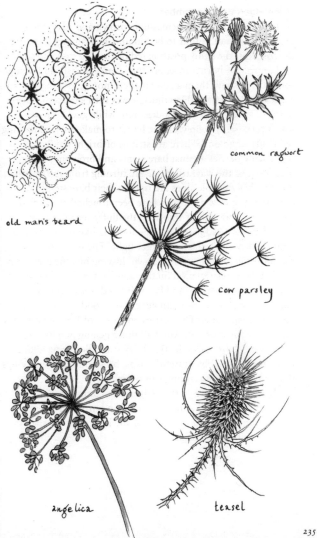

old man's beard

common ragwort

cow parsley

angelica

teasel

THE FLOWER GARDEN

November's flower garden picking prompts
A few heads of teasel from the roadside; a bunch of rosehips, crab apples, spindle and old man's beard; a little glass of winter pansies or violas.

Jobs in the flower garden

- This is the best month for planting tulips – any earlier and they can start into growth before the cold sets in, leaving them vulnerable over winter. Fill pots with them for flanking entryways, and plant bulbs direct into borders, too. Tulip 'Greenland' has pink petals with a striped green back and is upliftingly spring-like, while tulip 'China Pink' is a slightly stronger, clear pink with an elegant 'lily-flowered' shape.
- Shrubby roses always flower on new growth, so there is no harm at all in cutting them back now (unless they are still sporting hips, in which case you can leave them until late winter). Cut back about two thirds of the growth, cutting just above an outward-pointing bud each time, to encourage it to grow with an open structure next spring.
- If you plant paperwhite narcissi in pots indoors around the middle of the month, they should be in flower around Christmas. Stagger planting over this month if you want to be sure. Plant up forced hyacinths at the same time for early-winter flowers and scent.

THE KITCHEN GARDEN

Bare-root fruit bushes and trees become available in November, and this is the best time to plant them: you will get the best choice of varieties and they will establish well. Sow pea seeds thickly into a pot under cover for 'pea tips', harvested when they are just 8cm or so high and a welcome winter salad ingredient. You can also sow a crop of hardy peas outside but under a cloche to try to get a super-early crop next year. Mound up your Brussels sprouts to prevent them from rocking around in winter winds (and start picking them after the first frosts).

Sowing and planting crops

Fruit/veg	Sow under cover	Sow direct	Plant
Broad beans	✓	✓	
Garlic			✓
Pea tips	✓		
Peas	✓	✓	
Rhubarb			✓
Apple trees			✓
Pear trees			✓
Cherry trees			✓
Plum trees			✓
Raspberries			✓
Blackberries			✓
Currants			✓
Blueberries			✓
Figs			✓
Gooseberries			✓
Grapevines			✓
Peaches and nectarines			✓

N

THE KITCHEN

Sauce of the month – *bagna cauda*

This hot anchovy sauce is traditionally served in a bowl over a lit flame with vegetable crudités to dip in. Make a colourful plate of endive leaves, batons of carrot and turnip, and florets of cauliflower for cosy sharing.

Gently heat 125ml extra virgin olive oil in a small pan with four cloves of crushed garlic and 12 anchovies. Cook and stir for a few minutes. Cut 120g butter into cubes and drop in a cube at a time, whisking as it melts to create a creamy consistency. Repeat with the rest of the butter, a cube or two at a time, and when all is combined remove from the heat and whisk some more. Pour into a warmed bowl or into a fondue dish over a lit flame, then gather round and dip in immediately.

In season

Vegetables: Jerusalem artichokes, carrots, beetroot, turnips, swede, winter radishes, leeks, parsnips, cauliflowers, Brussels sprouts, kale, kohlrabi, winter cabbages, celeriac, celery, lettuces, endive, spinach, salad leaves, Oriental leaves, Swiss chard, stored maincrop potatoes, borlotti beans and winter squash

Herbs: chervil, parsley, coriander, sage, rosemary, bay

Fruit and nuts: apples, pears, medlars, quince, raspberries, imported cranberries, satsumas, clementines, pomegranates, hazelnuts, sweet chestnuts, walnuts

Fungi: all edible wild mushrooms, white truffles

Meat: duck, goose, grouse, guinea fowl, partridge, pheasant, venison, wood pigeon

Fish: brill, sardine, skate, clams, mussels, oysters

RECIPES

Rosehip syrup

Even if it weren't such a gorgeous ingredient, we could all do with a dose of rosehip syrup as winter sets in. Ludicrously rich in vitamin C, flavonoids, tannins and antioxidants, it is brilliant for warding off colds. However, it can also be poured over ice cream, made into sorbets or used in cocktails (see recipe on page 240) – the best way to keep germs at bay.

Makes about 1 litre
Ingredients
1kg rosehips, stalks removed
Granulated sugar (around 500g)

Method

Sterilise two 500ml bottles and their stoppers. Have 1 litre of water boiling in a large pan. In batches, put the rosehips into a blender with enough cold water to cover them, and blitz until they are cut up into small pieces. Immediately pour this into the boiling water. When all of the rosehips are in, bring to the boil and then simmer for 15 minutes. Lay two pieces of muslin on top of each other in a colander, and pour the liquid and pulp through it into a large bowl. Leave to drip through for 30 minutes, and then do the same again with two clean pieces of muslin. Measure or weigh the liquid, then return it to a clean pan with 325g sugar for every 500ml/500g liquid. Heat gently until the sugar has dissolved, then boil for 3 minutes. Decant into the bottles as soon as it is cool enough, label and store for up to 6 months.

N

Rosehip daiquiri

This cocktail contains all the elements of the classic daiquiri, plus the health-giving benefits of rosehips. (A shot is a standard cocktail measurement and equals about 3 tablespoons, or 45ml.)

Serves 1
Ingredients
¾ shot Rosehip Syrup (see page 239)
2 shots dark rum
1 shot lime juice
Ice cubes
Twist of lime, to garnish

Method
Shake the syrup, rum, lime juice and ice cubes together, then strain into a chilled coupe. Garnish each with a twist of lime.

CHARM OF THE MONTH

Pudding charms

The 22nd November is Stir-up Sunday, the day we must all get our puddings underway if they are to be suitably matured and brandy-soaked by Christmas Day. (It's a good day to make your Christmas cake and mincemeat, too, for the same reason.) This is the last Sunday before Advent, and the name comes from the beginning of the Anglican Church's prayer for the day: 'Stir up, we beseech thee, oh Lord, the wills of thy faithful people.' Of course this has nothing whatsoever to do with puddings, but a necessary task and a handily timed Bible reading have become conjoined over the years. A Christmas pudding should contain exactly 13 ingredients, to represent Jesus and the disciples. It should be stirred from east to west to represent the journey of the Magi. Each member of the family should stir it and make a wish as they do so. In what is thought to possibly be a hangover of far older charm traditions associated with Epiphany, silver charms were once included at this stage, and each represented a different facet of luck for the year ahead: a silver sixpence for wealth, a ring for love and marriage, and a thimble for luck.

A SONG FOR NOVEMBER'S FULL MOON

'Van Diemen's Land'
Traditional, arr. Richard Barnard

In this song our poor heroes set out under the moonlight to go poaching – a common but risky autumnal country pursuit when food was scarce – but are caught red-handed. The rest of the song follows their transportation to Australia's principal 19th-century penal colony, which was in Van Diemen's Land, as the Australian island of Tasmania was called then. Transportation was often the punishment for crimes as petty as stealing a loaf of bread, and this is one of a great many folk songs bewailing the unfairness of such an extreme punishment.

Come, all you gallant poachers that ramble free from care, that walk out on a moon-lit night with your dog and gun and snare, the hare and lofty pheasant that you have at your command, not thinking of your last career out on Van Diemen's Land.

Come, all you gallant poachers that ramble free from care,
That walk out on a moonlit night with your dog, and gun
and snare,
The hare and lofty pheasant you have at your command,
Not thinking of your last career out on Van Diemen's Land.

Me and two more went out one night to Squire Daniel's park,
To see if we could catch some game, the night it being dark,
But to our great misfortune we felt the keeper's hand,
Our sentence was for fourteen years upon Van Diemen's Land.

Oh, when we came to land there, upon that fatal shore,
The planters they came flocking round, full twenty score or more,
They ranked us up like horses and sold us out of hand,
They yoked us up with heavy chains to plough Van Deimen's
Land.

I often look behind me towards my native shore,
And dream of my old cottage that I shall see no more,
With my true love beside me and a jug of ale in hand,
But wake quite broken-hearted out in Van Diemen's Land.

So come, you gallant poachers, give ear unto my song,
It is a bit of good advice although it is not long,
Lay by your dog and snare, to you I do speak plain.
If you knew our great hardships, you'd never poach again.

N

December

- **1**   Start of meteorological winter

- **11**   11th–18th: Hannukah, festival of lights (Jewish) – begins at sunset on 10th

- **21**   Winter solstice, start of astronomical winter. Also known as Yule (pagan/neopagan) or Midwinter/Midwinter's Day

- **24**   Christmas Eve (Christian)

- **25**   Christmas Day (Christian)

- **26**   Boxing Day/St Stephen's Day (Christian)

- **28**   Bank holiday in lieu of Boxing Day, England, Scotland, Wales, Northern Ireland

- **31**   New Year's Eve

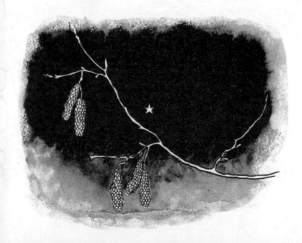

THE MOON

Names for December's full moon – Full Cold Moon, Oak Moon, Moon After Yule

December's Full Cold Moon is the highest and brightest of the year. In the year-round wrestle for dominion that is played out in the sky between the sun and the moon, the moon is definitely winning right now, and shines high, bright and strong over the winter countryside, just as the sun stays low and weak. But, of course, December brings the winter solstice, the moment at which the pendulum starts to swing back the other way. Neopagans believe that in pre-Christian times, the year was ruled over by two kings, the Holly King from the summer solstice to the winter solstice, and the Oak King, from winter to summer. They had to do battle for supremacy, and the winter solstice was the moment at which the Oak King slayed the Holly King and – like the sun – started to build strength. Perhaps this is some clue to the origin of the name Oak Moon. This December's full moon falls after the solstice, and so it also takes the name Moon After Yule.

Moon phases

3rd quarter – *8th December, 00.37*

New moon – *14th December, 16.17*

1st quarter – *21st December, 23.41*

Full moon – *30th December, 03.28*

Moonrise and set

	Lowestoft		*Dunquin*		
	Rise	Set	Rise	Set	
1st	16.25	08.42	17.17	09.31	
2nd	17.08	09.45	18.01	10.34	
3rd	18.04	10.40	18.57	11.28	
4th	19.10	11.24	20.03	12.12	
5th	20.24	11.58	21.17	12.46	
6th	21.43	12.24	22.35	13.13	
7th	23.03	12.46	23.56	13.35	
8th	–	13.04	–	13.53	3rd quarter
9th	00.25	13.21	01.17	14.11	
10th	01.49	13.38	02.40	14.28	
11th	03.15	13.57	04.06	14.47	
12th	04.43	14.19	05.34	15.10	
13th	06.13	14.48	07.03	15.39	
14th	07.39	15.26	08.29	16.18	new moon
15th	08.57	16.18	09.46	17.11	
16th	09.59	17.22	10.47	18.16	
17th	10.45	18.36	11.33	19.30	
18th	11.18	19.54	12.06	20.47	
19th	11.42	21.10	12.31	22.02	
20th	12.01	22.34	12.50	23.15	
21st	12.17	23.34	13.05	–	1st quarter
22nd	12.30	–	13.20	00.26	
23rd	12.44	00.43	13.33	01.34	
24th	12.58	01.51	13.47	02.42	
25th	13.13	03.00	14.03	03.50	
26th	13.31	04.09	14.22	05.00	
27th	13.54	05.20	14.45	06.09	
28th	14.24	06.29	15.16	07.19	
29th	15.04	07.35	15.56	08.24	
30th	15.56	08.34	16.49	09.23	full moon
31st	17.00	09.22	17.53	10.11	

Where moonset times are before moonrise times, this is the setting of the previous night's moon.

Gardening by the moon

Full moon to 3rd quarter: 1st–8th and 30th–31st. Harvest crops for immediate eating. Harvest fruit.

3rd quarter to new moon: 8th–14th. Prune. Harvest for storage. Fertilise and mulch the soil.

New moon to 1st quarter: 14th–21st. Sow crops that develop below ground. Dig the soil.

1st quarter to full moon: 21st–30th. Sow crops that develop above ground. Plant seedlings and young plants.

December moon dates

14th and 30th – new moon and full moon: best fishing days.
Some fishermen believe that fish bite best in the 45 minutes either side of moonrise and set on the new and full moons. So that would be 90 minutes from 06.54 and 14.41 on the 14th, and from 07.49 and 15.11 on the 30th (Lowestoft times).

15th – new moon in Sagittarius. This month's new moon is in freedom-loving Sagittarius, and astrologers believe this is a time for dreaming about travel and also for planning studies. You will see the fruits of this around the Sagittarius full moon on 26th May 2021.

16th – day after the calculated first sighting of the new crescent moon: the start of Tevet. The third day of the Jewish month of Tevet – this year 18th December – brings the end of Hannukah, the Jewish festival of lights.

16th (predicted) – day after the sighting of the new crescent moon: the start of Jumada al-Awwal. Jumada al-Awwal is the fifth month of the Islamic year.

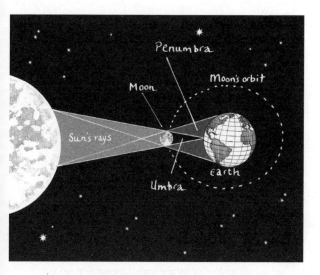

Solar eclipse

Total solar eclipses are not hugely rare, but unlike lunar eclipses – which the whole night-time world can see – they have a small and specific path. Sadly, there were no total eclipses in the British Isles in 2020, but on the 14th of this month one will be visible in southern Africa, South America and – helpfully – parts of the Pacific, Atlantic and Indian Oceans.

A total eclipse occurs when the new moon moves directly between the earth and the sun, and it is the one moment we can truly appreciate one of the great cosmic coincidences: that from earth the sun and the moon appear exactly the same size. The sun is 400 times larger than the moon, and it is also 400 times farther away from us – if it were just slightly nearer, total solar eclipses would never happen. Because the moon is smaller than the earth and far away, its shadow, or the 'area of totality', falls on just a small section of the earth, and so only those on the tips of the southern continents – and an awful lot of fishes – will experience it this time.

THE SKY

At night

12th Close approach of the moon and Venus, visible low in the southeastern sky from about 06.00 until 07.30.

13th–14th The impressive Geminids meteor shower is caused by debris from Asteroid 3200 Phaethon burning up in the earth's atmosphere. The radiant (see page 16) reaches an altitude of 70 degrees in the south at 02.00 – viewing should be good for a few hours before and after this.

17th Close approach of the moon, Jupiter and Saturn, visible in the dusk from 16.00 in the south until setting in the southwest at 18.00. Maximum altitude of 15 degrees.

21st Very close approach (0.1 degrees) of Jupiter and Saturn, visible in the dusk from 16.00 at an altitude of 14 degrees until setting at 17.30 in the southwest.

23rd–24th Close approach of the moon and Mars, visible from 16.00 in the southeast until 01.30 in the west.

By day

The winter solstice falls on 21st December at 10.02, when the North Pole is at its maximum tilt (23.44 degrees) away from the sun. The sun will be overhead at the tropic of Capricorn.

The sun reaches an altitude of 15 degrees in the London sky and 11 degrees in the Glasgow sky at solar midday on the winter solstice on 21st December.

Day length decreases by 22m in Lowestoft, Suffolk, and by 21m in Dunquin, Republic of Ireland, and then increases by 6m in Lowestoft and by 5m in Dunquin.

Latest sunrise: 30th December, Lowestoft 08.03, Dunquin 08.50.

Earliest sunset: 12/13th December, Lowestoft 15.38, 12th December, Dunquin 16.29.

Sunrise and set

	Lowestoft		*Dunquin*	
	Rise	Set	Rise	Set
1st	07.41	15.42	08.28	16.33
2nd	07.42	15.41	08.29	16.32
3rd	07.44	15.41	08.31	16.31
4th	07.45	15.40	08.32	16.31
5th	07.46	15.40	08.33	16.30
6th	07.48	15.40	08.35	16.30
7th	07.49	15.39	08.36	16.30
8th	07.50	15.39	08.37	16.29
9th	07.51	15.39	08.38	16.29
10th	07.52	15.38	08.39	16.29
11th	07.53	15.38	08.40	16.29
12th	07.54	15.38	08.41	16.29
13th	07.55	15.38	08.42	16.29
14th	07.56	15.38	08.43	16.29
15th	07.57	15.39	08.44	16.29
16th	07.58	15.39	08.45	16.29
17th	07.59	15.39	08.46	16.30
18th	07.59	15.39	08.46	16.30
19th	08.00	15.40	08.47	16.30
20th	08.00	15.40	08.47	16.31
21st	08.01	15.41	08.48	16.31
22nd	08.01	15.41	08.48	16.32
23rd	08.02	15.42	08.49	16.32
24th	08.02	15.42	08.49	16.33
25th	08.03	15.43	08.50	16.34
26th	08.03	15.44	08.50	16.35
27th	08.03	15.45	08.50	16.35
28th	08.03	15.46	08.50	16.36
29th	08.03	15.46	08.50	16.37
30th	08.03	15.47	08.50	16.38
31st	08.03	15.48	08.50	16.39

D

THE SEA

Average sea temperature

Ayr:	10.2°C
Sunderland:	9.0°C
Dingle:	11.1°C
Dublin:	11.3°C
Aberystwyth:	10.9°C
Lowestoft:	10.2°C
Poole:	11.9°C
Newquay:	11.8°C

Spring and neap tides

The spring tides are the most extreme tides of the month, with the highest rises and falls, and the neap tides are the least extreme, with the smallest. Exact timings vary around the coast, but expect them around the following dates:

Spring tides: 1st–2nd and 15th–16th

Neap tides: 8th–9th and 22nd–23rd

In the tide timetable opposite, spring tides are shown with an asterisk.

December tide timetable for Dover

For guidance on how to convert this for your local area, see page 8.

| | *High water* | | *Low water* | |
	Morning	Afternoon	Morning	Afternoon
1st*	11.22	23.41	06.23	18.40
2nd*	11.50	–	06.57	19.14
3rd	00.08	12.20	07.31	19.47
4th	00.39	12.53	08.07	20.22
5th	01.16	13.33	08.44	20.59
6th	02.01	14.23	09.26	21.43
7th	02.57	15.27	10.16	22.37
8th	04.10	16.59	11.21	23.50
9th	05.32	18.23	–	12.39
10th	06.45	19.26	01.13	13.51
11th	07.46	20.21	02.23	14.54
12th	08.40	21.12	03.25	15.56
13th	09.31	22.00	04.25	16.57
14th	10.20	22.46	05.22	17.53
15th*	11.07	23.31	06.15	18.44
16th*	11.53	–	07.04	19.30
17th	00.16	12.39	07.50	20.13
18th	01.01	13.25	08.34	20.54
19th	01.47	14.13	09.18	21.34
20th	02.35	15.04	10.02	22.15
21st	03.25	15.58	10.48	23.01
22nd	04.19	16.59	11.41	23.58
23rd	05.20	18.07	–	12.39
24th	06.26	19.15	01.03	13.40
25th	07.31	20.11	02.07	14.37
26th	08.25	20.58	03.05	15.30
27th	09.09	21.38	03.57	16.18
28th	09.48	22.14	04.42	17.01
29th	10.24	22.49	05.23	17.42
30th	11.00	23.23	06.02	18.22
31st	11.35	23.57	06.42	19.01

NATURE

The hedgerow in December

This is the time of the long sleeps, when the hedgerow inhabitants have tucked themselves back underground or into nooks out of harm's way. The hedgerow's greatest contribution to the lives of its inhabitants now is in creating shelter, filtering winds, sloughing off some of the rains and forming sunny little enclaves at its base. On cold days you would think that nothing lives in it (though you would be grateful to be standing on the leeward side of it). However, on milder days there can be some tentative venturing out in search of sustenance. Seven-spotted ladybirds will rouse themselves from their crannies and creep along branches on the hunt for overwintering aphids, and badgers will go out foraging whenever there is a decent spell. Even hedgehogs will come out of deepest hibernation and move to a new spot, snuffling for grubs along the way.

You have to look hard for signs of life, but hazel catkins are already starting to fatten and elongate: spring is having ideas even in the depths of winter. Old man's beard is now shedding those fluffy seeds, and they are being lifted by winter winds to drift and hopefully fall on bare ground, where they will wait patiently to germinate in warmer times. Spindle likewise has dropped its orange seeds to take their chances, leaving just the pink wings of the casings dangling prettily. Holly berries are shiny and red against the dark foliage, begging to be plucked by birds or by human foragers. Ivy – always keeping its own time and still producing flowers even in these darkest moments – is just starting to turn some of those flowers to black berries, which will be loved by the birds as the hedgerow heads deeper into winter.

THE FLOWER GARDEN

December's flower garden picking prompts

A spray of winter jasmine, ivy foliage and ivy flowers (if tied with a ribbon, this can also double as a festive door decoration); a single sprig of something winter-flowering to scent the house, such as chimomanthus, sarcococca or witch hazel; a lichen-covered branch and a branch of berried cotoneaster, perhaps hung with delicate baubles or silvery lametta (tinsel emulating icicles).

Jobs in the flower garden

- Once dahlias have been blackened by frost, it is time to lift them and store them away for the hardest parts of winter. Brush off the worst of the soil, let them dry out for a couple of weeks, and then pack them into moist sand, to prevent them shrivelling. In mild areas you can leave them in the ground, but mulch them thickly to protect them from frost.

- A dry and mild December, should we get one, is a good time for planting evergreen shrubs. If you have found you have no access to berried holly in the run-up to Christmas, this would be a good time to remedy it for future years. *Ilex aquifolium* 'J C Van Tol' produces good red berries, while 'Golden Van Tol' is much the same but with a gold edge to the foliage. *Ilex aquifolium* 'Amber' has unusual orange berries.

- Likewise, if you don't have any ivy in your garden to twine around your banisters and run along your mantelpiece, plant some now – as long as the ground isn't frozen – and you will have plenty next year. Some people consider ivy a pest, but it can soften hard landscaping beautifully and you can keep it in check by pulling out great reams of it around midwinter every year.

D

THE KITCHEN GARDEN

Prepare beds for next year by digging or just by weeding them and covering with manure. They will be ready to plant into next spring. Lift and divide rhubarb crowns that have got large and congested, replanting with some fresh compost. As long as the ground isn't frozen, this is another good month for fruit tree planting if you didn't manage it last month. Winter prune your apple and pear trees.

Sowing and planting crops

Fruit/veg	Sow under cover	Sow direct	Plant
Broad beans	✓	✓	
Garlic			✓
Rhubarb			✓
Apple trees			✓
Pear trees			✓
Cherry trees			✓
Plum trees			✓
Raspberries			✓
Blackberries			✓
Currants			✓
Blueberries			✓
Figs			✓
Gooseberries			✓
Grape vines			✓
Peaches and nectarines			✓

THE KITCHEN

Sauce of the month – gravy

You will need to have made (or bought) a good stock beforehand, by taking the carcass or bones of a previous roast and simmering them for at least two hours with a quartered onion (skin on, for colour), a chopped carrot and a bay leaf or two.

While roasting the bird or joint that this gravy will be accompanying, put a finely diced onion and a sprig of rosemary in a frying pan with a big knob of butter and cook them low and slow until the onions are translucent (you could also do this ahead of time and keep it in the fridge). When you remove the bird or joint from the oven for it to rest, tip the juices into a jug. They will separate, and you can take a few tablespoons of the fat from the surface and put them back into the roasting tray. Put the tray on the heat, then tip in the fried onion and rosemary along with two heaped tablespoons of flour, and cook for a few minutes. The flour will start to brown, and this is a good thing as it will help with the colour of your gravy. Tip in a glass of white wine and mix thoroughly, using it to scrape all of the browned bits from the pan. It will thicken considerably, but you need to let it bubble for a minute or two to cook off the alcohol. Start to add the meat juices (spoon off the fat first) a little at a time, and the stock, until you have the amount and thickness you want. The longer you can let it bubble, the browner it will get. Season with salt and pepper, and serve piping hot.

In season

Vegetables: Jerusalem artichokes, carrots, beetroot, leeks, parsnips, swede, celeriac, endive, winter radishes, cauliflowers, Brussels sprouts, kale, winter cabbages, stored maincrop potatoes, borlotti beans, winter squash

Herbs: chervil, parsley, coriander, sage, rosemary, bay

Fruits and nuts: stored apples, pears, quince, imported cranberries, satsumas, clementines, pomegranates, hazelnuts, sweet chestnuts, walnuts

Fungi: black truffles

D

CHARM OF THE MONTH

The wishbone

After Christmas dinner, the turkey's wishbone – the V-shaped bone above its breastbone – is taken out, cleaned and left to dry, which will be faster if placed by the fire. As soon as it is nicely dried out, it is ready to be used. Two people – usually chosen from the children at the table – face off, make a wish and wrap their pudgy pinkies around a side each, then pull until it snaps. The one left holding the longest end wins, and their wish will come true (this is thought to be the origin of the term 'lucky break'). Traditions around the wishbone are found in many cultures. Prussian and Celtic armies used wishbones to predict the weather, and the ancient Etruscans once used the movements and bones of birds for divination, and would dry out the wishbone and stroke it while making wishes. The Romans took the tradition from the Etruscans and spread it around their empire. In Britain the bone took on (and later lost) the name 'merrythought' and became part of the Christmas ritual. Eventually it went across the Atlantic to the United States, where there are, of course, plentiful wild turkeys. Although in the US the turkey, along with its wishbone, is principally connected with Thanksgiving, in the UK it has become most strongly associated with the Christmas turkey.

EDIBLE CLAMS

pod razor

european flat oyster

queen scallop

blue mussel

sea cockle

RECIPES

Pepper cake, for carollers

Pepper cake is a dark, treacly, spicy fruitcake that was made in the Lake District around Christmas time specifically for feeding to calling carollers. There is disagreement as to whether it contained actual pepper or whether 'pepper' was just a synonym for spice, but this one contains it along with other spices. You don't taste the pepper particularly, but it imparts its warmth.

Makes 12 slices
Ingredients
75g raisins
75g currants
75g butter
150ml water
100g golden caster sugar
225g black treacle
225g self-raising flour
½ teaspoon ground ginger
Large pinch ground cloves
¼ teaspoon finely ground black pepper
¼ a freshly grated nutmeg
4 tablespoons milk
1 egg, beaten

Method
Grease and line an 18cm cake tin with baking parchment. Preheat the oven to 180°C, Gas Mark 4. Put the fruit, butter and water in a saucepan, bring to the boil, and simmer for 10 minutes. Remove from the heat and stir in the sugar and black treacle, then leave to cool for 10 minutes. Put the flour

and spices into a large bowl, and pour in the fruit mixture
and the milk and beaten egg. Mix thoroughly and tip into the
cake tin. Bake for about 50 minutes, or until a skewer pushed
into the centre comes out clean and hot. Leave the cake to cool
completely, and eat it spread with butter, or with a slice of
cheese, or on its own with a glass of Ginger Cordial (see below).

Ginger cordial, for carollers

Along with pepper cake, carollers were traditionally given a
glass of hot ginger cordial, to warm their vocal cords.

Makes 1 litre

Ingredients

8cm piece of root ginger, peeled and grated

Thinly pared zest and juice of 1 lemon

600g golden caster sugar

1.5 litres water

15g citric acid

Method

Sterilise two 500ml bottles with caps. Place the ginger in a large
saucepan with the lemon zest and juice, sugar and water. Heat
gently, stirring, until the sugar has completely dissolved, then
bring to a gentle boil. Boil for about 40 minutes, until the liquid
has turned syrupy. Stir in the citric acid and then leave to sit,
covered, overnight. In the morning, strain through a muslin
into the sterilised bottles. Seal with the caps and use within
6 months.

For hot ginger cordial, put a few centimetres of the cordial
in the base of a cup, and top with boiling water. You might add
a splash of whisky, too.

A SONG FOR DECEMBER'S FULL MOON

'The Moon Shines Bright'
Traditional, arr. Richard Barnard

This beautiful old country carol was originally collected by folk song collector Lucy Broadwood from gypsy singers in Suffolk and Surrey around 1900, and is thought to have medieval origins. It was most likely sung by wassailers, who went from house to house like today's carol singers.

The moon shines bright and the stars give a light
A little before the day.
The Lord our God, he calls on us
And bids us awake and pray.

So for the saving of our souls
Christ died upon the cross.
We ne'er shall do for Jesus Christ
What he has done for us.

The life of man, it is but a span
And cut down like a flower.
For he's here today, but tomorrow he is gone
And dead all in an hour.

The clock strikes one, and it's time we were gone,
We'll stay no longer here.
God bless you all, both great and small
And send you a happy New Year.

REFERENCES

Astronomical events based on ephemerides obtained using the NASA
    JPL Horizons system
Calendarial and astronomical information reproduced with permission
    from HMNAO, UKHO and the Controller of Her Majesty's
    Stationery Office
Moon and sun rises and sets and related calculations reproduced with
    permission from www.timeanddate.com
Tidal predictions reproduced with permission from HMNAO, UKHO
    and the Controller of Her Majesty's Stationery Office.
Sea temperatures reproduced with permission from www.
    seatemperatures.org

ACKNOWLEDGEMENTS

Thanks to my dad, Jack Leendertz, who plays a huge part in helping me to pull together the astronomical information in *The Almanac* each year, and who this year was called upon to check and correct the moon content as well.

I am delighted to include recipe contributions from MiMi Aye (author of *Mandalay: Recipe and Tales from a Burmese Kitchen*), Yemisi Aribisala (author of *Longthroat Memoirs: Soup, Sex and Nigerian Taste Buds*) and Irina Georgescu (author of the upcoming *Carpathia: Food from the Heart of Romania*), which have provided glimpses into the annual food traditions of the UK's Burmese, Nigerian and Romanian communities. Thank you all for enriching *The Almanac* with your wonderful ideas, knowledge and recipes.

Thank you to Angela Morris and Tim Homewood of Homewood Cheeses for permission to use your Pasha recipe, and to Julia Jones for permission to use your Suffolk Fourses Cake from the brilliant *Cattern Cakes and Lace*.

Richard Barnard has worked meticulously on the folk songs, unearthing and researching many versions and in places putting his own spin on them in the true folk tradition. Thank you Richard for such careful and creative work.

Thank you to Robin Heath (www.skyandlandscape.com/ www.robinheath.info) for permission to make our own copy of his diagram 'The Tock of the Moon' from *Sun, Moon & Earth* (Wooden Books).

One of the great delights of creating each edition of *The Almanac* is finding and working alongside a new illustrator, and it has been a joy working with Julia McKenzie this year. Thank you, Julia, for your delicate and atmospheric work and for bringing the seasons alive so beautifully.

Thank you as ever to designer Matt Cox of Newman + Eastwood for bringing calm, beautiful order to the potential chaos of my ideas. And thank you to the whole brilliant team at Octopus: Stephanie Jackson, Jonathan Christie, Ella Parsons, Matt Grindon, Karen Baker and Kevin Hawkins. Thanks also to Alison Wormleighton and Jane Birch, and to my agent, the excellent Adrian Sington at Kruger Cowne.

And finally, thanks to my mum and John for all your practical and emotional support, and huge love and thanks to Michael, Rowan and Meg, just for being you, you gorgeous, lovely things.

INDEX

ABOUT THE AUTHOR

Lia Leendertz is an award-winning garden and food writer based in Bristol. She writes regularly for the *Telegraph*, *The Garden*, *Simple Things*, the *Guardian* and *Gardens Illustrated*. Her reinvention of the traditional rural almanac has become an annual must-have for readers eager to connect with the seasons, appreciate the outdoors and discover ways to mark and celebrate each month. Now established as the bestselling almanac in the market, this is the third instalment.

Find out more about Lia at:
www.lialeendertz.com
🐦 @lialeendertz
📷 @lia_leendertz

ABOUT THE ILLUSTRATOR

Julia McKenzie is an artist from South London who creates drawings, collages and prints. Her work explores the natural world, often in relation to her urban environment. Birds, plants, insects and objects combine to create complex narratives. Julia's clients include the Imperial War Museum in London, and the British Library has collected her work.

Find out more about Julia at:
www.juliamckenzie.co.uk
📷 @mckenzie_julia

CALENDAR 2020

JULY

M	T	W	T	F	S	S
		1	2	3	4	5
6	7	8	9	10	11	12
13	14	15	16	17	18	19
20	21	22	23	24	25	26
27	28	29	30	31		

SEPTEMBER

M	T	W	T	F	S	S
	1	2	3	4	5	6
7	8	9	10	11	12	13
14	15	16	17	18	19	20
21	22	23	24	25	26	27
28	29	30				

NOVEMBER

M	T	W	T	F	S	S
						1
2	3	4	5	6	7	8
9	10	11	12	13	14	15
16	17	18	19	20	21	22
23	24	25	26	27	28	29
30						